'I wish I had read this when I was seventeen and again at thirty-five.'

- Professor Mercy Amba Oduyoye
Director, Institute of Women in Religion & Culture
Trinity Theological Seminary

'Two words jumped at me when I went through Broken for Use: Divine Potter! Yes, God our Divine Potter is patient, diligent, tender and yet firm and relentless. God has one purpose - to make us as He desires and that is exactly what He has done with Reverend Akua Buabema Ofori Boateng. The end product is beautiful and useful.
You must read this book.'

- The Reverend Dr. Joyce Aryee
Executive Director, Salt and Light Ministries

'Broken for Use is a moving personal and spiritual memoir which is vulnerable in bold letters. It is for those who are comfortable with their humanity, and always grateful for the extent of the grace of God in their lives. Filled with instances of God's grace working in human depravity, the author demonstrates that our deepest purpose and truest destination can only be fulfilled by God's calling on our lives. I wholeheartedly recommend it for all sinners saved by grace.'

- The Reverend Dr. Casely B. Essamuah
Secretary, Global Christian Forum

'In this candid and engaging account, Akua Ofori-Boateng reveals how an especially harrowing time leads to the more exceptional discovery of her life   ....ring does not sufficiently describe Aku;

- Pakw
Entre

BROKEN FOR USE

Reverend Akua Buabema Ofori-Boateng

FOREWORD BY

PROFESSOR MERCY AMBA ODUYOYE

ISBN: 978-9988-53-591-9

Published by Aequitas
Contact info: info@aequitasfoundation.org
+233 (0)54 541 1414

Typesetting by RONEL Ghana Limited
Contact info: hello@ronelagency.com
+233 (0)55 518 8889

Cover Design by RONEL Ghana Limited
Contact info: hello@ronelagency.com
+233 (0)55 518 8889

Printed by Buck Press Limited
Contact info: buck@buckpress.com
+233 (0)30 240 8061

DEDICATION

To

The memory of my late father, Josiah Ofori-Boateng,

My mother, Sabina Ofori-Boateng

and

My priest, Reverend Canon Samuel Lanquaye Lamptey

APPRECIATION

I am exceedingly grateful to Professor Mercy Amba Oduyoye (Aunty Mercy) for graciously agreeing to write the Foreword.

The following are the good Samaritans without whom this book would not have been possible. To you I say thank you!

Oduma Agyei
Kwesi Amoak
Matilda Amissah-Arthur
Ama Gyamfuaa Awua-Kyerematen
Julius Osei Appiah
Rami Baitie
Abena Darfoor
Professor Alexander Dodoo
Paul Anthony Rahman Issah Dowuona
Judith Fang
Denis Goodman
Florence Christine Maame Ekua Hagan
Francis Kwao
David Lawson
Diana Lecosson
Very Reverend George Kotei Neequaye
Nana Addo Nhyira-Addo
Elizabeth Ohene
Kwaku Sakyi-Addo
Romal Tune

However, as it is written:
"What no eye has seen,
 what no ear has heard,
and what no human mind has conceived"
 the things God has prepared for those who love him

1 Corinthians 2:9 (NIV)

CONTENTS

AUTHOR'S NOTE

The following names, listed in alphabetical order are pseudonyms: Angela, Mr. Arthur, Barry, Brian, Chris, Evelyn, Gabriella, Idris, James, Jacob, Joseph, Judah, Judith, Jürgen, Nathaniel, Pierre, Rasheed, Richard, Samson, Sebastian, Seth, Silas, Tamara, and Thomas.

FOREWORD

Before you read the book in your hand read this!

I received the manuscript just before our focus became COVID-19. I had something in hand so I said I could not get to this before the end of April and the author said it would be fine. I put the manuscript aside and went on with my 'academic task'. But I could not forget the title of the tome I had put on the back burner 'Broken for Use'. After two days I dropped the work in hand, picked it up and did not put it away until I had finished reading it, and I mean reading, not scanning. Then I said to myself, I wish I had read this when I was seventeen and again at thirty-five. This is a message for young people, but even as an octogenarian, I knew I had to read it again. In this preface I share with you some of the many gems that I picked up as I read Broken for Use.

First is the role Scripture plays in the telling of her *simple truth*. While you are reading, note how she picked the most apt Bible verses, some 96 of them to enrich her thoughts. Akua is asking you to read the Bible for yourself so you do not miss God's Word speaking directly into your situation. This book, as the author says, is about the power of God, not about Akua Buabema; but you are bound to learn from her intimacy with God as I did. In our contemporary parlance, this is a motivational speech that spans eleven chapters of a hundred and eighty-six pages of an A4 manuscript, and warns you that being 'grown' does not mean you are 'mature', neither does being 'broken' mean you are useless.

Akua "graduated from secondary school bitter and hurt but also in love…grown but not mature." After many pages and many years through wildernesses and betrayals, she still wishes to let you know that while she was "educated, well-employed, married and a mother…yet something felt off" Does that sound familiar? Well, read on.

My reading led me to a core word, **APPROVAL**. Discover this, search your own heart and you will agree with Akua that there is wisdom in 'trying to be happy without external approval'. My reading gave me a whole A4 notes on this theme of approval, on the need to be counted cool, needing other people to validate your existence and your doings. Self-pity, self-hate, lack of self-confidence, lack of self-esteem. The addiction to approval is what keeps us doing all we can do "to keep being relevant and appreciated by others." Search for and watch the interview recorded in chapter six.

You never know what others appreciate in you and as a friend told her, you may be the only Bible they will ever read. She alerts us on the state of feeling inadequate and not worthy of love because of your physical appearance.

Akua's take on marriage is wisdom for all women, young and old, and I dare say, for all marriage counsellors too. Her reading of Proverbs 31 is worth visiting as she underlines the fact that the woman under scrutiny in the chapter, beloved of wedding preachers and whom we should know, is a "wonderfully amazing woman, an individual", a model of security and of a sense of self-worth. Those who feel "incomplete and inadequate before marriage and motherhood" will benefit from a reading of 'Broken For Use'.

One more thing, many live in and with fear of offending companions, others fear the terrible out bursts some are able to generate at the drop of a hat just to get their way. Some of us can say, "everything in my life revolves around fear, fear of the devil, witches, being cursed, being under ancestral curse, being taken advantage of, and many others".

When we are young, it could be fear of what our parents would do to us if we 'messed' up. This, and the fear of God, may keep you on the straight and narrow. But my take on this is, doing so because you love yourself, your parents and your God who first loved you, is a healthier fear. Other fears simply steal your joy and peace. There are the weapons of naysayers, who take joy in preying on your misery. Some actually do so because they benefit from 'praying' for your 'prosperity'. Only God holds your future. Like Jesus, we can each resurrect from our struggles, but we have to walk with our hands firmly in God's, our "True North".

The child of God who gave me this to read came to my house an ordinary young woman who later turned out to be one of the youngsters I might have met around Onyasia Crescent, Roman Ridge in the mid-1990s. Later, in the space of twenty hours, I was to see and hear her on TV in the persona of a sophisticated corporate woman and later a 'cassocked' handmaiden, a person of the cloth. By then I had finished reading her manuscript, although I had told her a week before I would not be able to get to it before the end of April.

Having met her at Professor John S. Pobee's "send off" vespers, identified by two of Roman Ridge's youngsters, and having heard her personally when she came to deliver the work, there was no way I was going to lay it aside from mid-March to end of April.

By the time she paid me a fleeting visit the next Sunday, bringing me a hand sanitizer, I had finished my first reading and had put myself under discipline to not touch it again until I had completed the "academic exercise" I had in hand, which I also love doing.

All I am saying is that this book is a must read if only for its status as a well written, pleasant to read narrative, replete with apt biblical references.

"Broken for Use" is the "Simple Truth" of a woman who knew herself to be under the guidance of God, who had God as a friend and begged, bargained, cajoled, but kept listening for, and as is often with religious experience, kept seeing God after God had passed by.

Read, enjoy, ponder, and who knows, you too may recognize God accompanying you.

Professor Mercy Amba Oduyoye
Director, Institute of Women in Religion & Culture
Trinity Theological Seminary

INTRODUCTION

**And they have defeated him by the blood of the Lamb
and by their testimony.
Revelation 12:11 (NLT)**

P ain and shame affect us all. It can be the pain from the death of a loved one, or the shame we experience by virtue of our own failure and sin. Whatever the cause, we can all identify with pain and shame at some level and it can feel like we have been broken.

But being "broken" does not mean being useless. We are never too far gone to be healed and redeemed by God. Where we struggle, God will strengthen us. And when we fail, God will restore us.

And in our restoration, God uses us to speak into the lives of other "broken" people. Our life experiences become the bandages upon which He pours the ointments of grace and mercy and power, and uses them to bring healing and comfort to others.

> **But we have this treasure in jars of clay to show that this all-surpassing power is from God and not from us. 2 Corinthians 4:7 (NIV)**

This is a story about the power of God. It is not intended to condemn anyone, nor to place anyone on a pedestal. It is *my simple truth*, about how the goodness of God shines through our brokenness.

Akua Ofori-Boateng

CHAPTER ONE

GOD HAS ALWAYS KNOWN

**Before I formed you in the womb I knew you, before
you were born I set you apart; I appointed you as a
prophet to the nations.
Jeremiah 1:5 (NIV)**

I was eight when I first experienced God in a tangible way.
It was one month to my eighth birthday and four months
before I would go to my next class, Class 4.

In Class 4, I would become a senior. This was particularly
important to me because as a senior in Ridge Church School, a
Christian elementary school, I needed to have a "big people's"
Bible. Specifically, I needed a Good News Bible.

This was in 1984. And Ghana at that time was a place of
shortages. A military coup had overthrown the government in
1981 and the socio-economic situation had left the country in a
state of shortage of most goods and commodities. There was a
shortage of everything. Everything, including Good News Bibles.
My mother had combed the whole city looking for one for me
with no luck. So one night, I decided I'd pray. Yes. My seven-year-
and-eleven-month old heart decided that God would provide my
answer. I had been told in school that God could do anything and
I believed that if I prayed, He would get me a Good News Bible.
So I prayed.

As a seven-year-old child, I did not fully understand the concept of a God who can do all things. However, even at that age, I had a strong sense of the presence of God in my life. I of course did not have a name or a term for that presence. It would be many years before I would come to realize that the presence I felt was the presence of the Holy Spirit.

My prayer was this "Dear God, I know Aunty Ruby is planning on bringing me a cake for my birthday. But I need a Good News Bible. Please give her a Good News Bible to bring to me, instead of a cake. In Jesus' name, Amen." That was my prayer. Short, simple and very clear. Or so I thought.

Aunty Ruby, my godmother, was a baker and there was an agreed routine for the celebrations of my birthdays. At 6:00 a.m. every morning on my birthday, she would show up with a lovely cake just for me. It had happened all my life and I knew she wouldn't fail me. But now it was up to God to switch the cake for a Bible.

I waited for what seemed like an eternity at the time. And then finally, the 26th of May showed up and at six in the morning, I heard it, "Beep! Beep!" Aunty Ruby's horn. I raced downstairs, my feet barely touching the floor. I just knew she was bringing me a Good News Bible. I had absolutely no doubt. After all, I had prayed for it. I saw her reach into the back of her car and lo and behold there it was…a wrapped book!

Wow! I was amazed! God actually heard my prayer. I gave her a quick hug and a kiss and left her to talk with my mom. With my gift in hand, I rushed to the dining table to unwrap it.

I ripped the wrapping off and, well…it was a Bible alright, but not a Good News Bible! It was an illustrated Children's Bible! I was dumbfounded. How could God have misunderstood? I was very specific. A GOOD NEWS BIBLE!! What could have gone wrong?

In my naïve disappointment, I thought God had not answered my prayer. What I did not know was that, He had in fact answered it beyond what I had asked for. It turned out He had understood my prayer better than I did. And two months later in July, this was made evident.

My oldest brother, Kofi, was a student at Ghana International School (GIS) and my parents had put in an application for me to go to the same school. But, as the premier school in the country at the time, it was very difficult to get into. So my parents were not surprised when after several weeks there had been no letter of acceptance for me from the school.

Then one day, I overheard my mother yelling at my brother. As the youngest child and the only girl, it was always fun to be around when my brothers were being chastised. I moved in closer to listen but not so close that I would become a casualty of my brother's misfortune. "How could you be so irresponsible?" I heard my mother yell.

It turned out that he had been given my acceptance letter to GIS sometime around my birthday in May but had forgotten it in his school bag. So my mother was chastising him because after two months, she was worried GIS would interpret not having received a response to the offer to mean that they were no longer interested in me attending the school. From my vantage point behind the dining room wall, I suddenly felt a coldness wash over me. I had goose bumps all over my body and I felt a pleasant warmth in my heart. At the time, I had no idea what it was.

Thirty years later in Seminary, I read an account from John Wesley about a similar feeling he experienced on 24th May 1738. He said,

"In the evening I went very unwillingly to a society in Aldersgate Street, where one was reading Luther's Preface to the Epistle to the Romans. About a quarter before nine, while he was describing the change which God works in the heart thro' faith in Christ, I felt my heart strangely warmed. I felt I did trust in Christ."

It made me think about what I felt when I was eight.

Naturally, as a child, I was only excited about having gained admission into GIS. I was not thinking about why I felt cold and warm hearted. It wasn't until that evening when I picked up my Children's Bible that it suddenly registered that God had not made a mistake at all with my birthday gift. He knew all along that I was going to go to GIS and that a Good News Bible would have been a waste. Given that GIS is a secular school, there was absolutely no need for a Bible as academic as the Good News Bible. I, of course, had no way of knowing about it then but the all-knowing God, to whom I prayed, knew beforehand that I was a GIS student even at the time I was praying for a Bible gift for my birthday.

He knew I would never have read that Bible. And He was right. What He gave me was a Bible that I would read and most importantly, a Bible that I would understand. What He gave me was a Bible that has formed the basis of my understanding of Scripture. That illustrated Children's Bible became the fertile soil upon which my comprehension of Scripture today was nurtured and has grown.

Today as a priest, despite the theological learning under my belt, when I think of Meshach, Shadrach and Abednego in the fire with a fourth figure, the image I have in my mind is the picture that was in my illustrated Children's Bible.

Many of us are disappointed in God because we've been so

explicit in expressing to Him exactly what we need from Him. It may be something serious like a child, marriage, school fees, or something as trivial as what I wanted. But whatever it is, God takes seriously our requests and has every intention of delivering what is absolutely best for us. But we must trust Him and never be disappointed in the outcome, no matter how different it is from what we expected.

> **Trust in the LORD with all your heart and lean not on your own understanding; in all your ways submit to him and he will make your paths straight. Proverbs 3:5-6 (NIV)**

Needless to say, this incident made a big impression on me. And it would be the start of a long but tumultuous relationship between God and myself. At that tender age of eight, I felt within me a very deep affection for God. I saw Him as a father figure and as a close older friend. Someone I could trust.

This birthday and the Bible gift would also mark the beginning of a new way with which I would make many of my life decisions. I started making decisions based on that gut feeling, that assuredness I felt on the day I received the Bible. I began to notice it more and more. And I realized I had felt it many times before but had ignored it because I didn't know what it was. The only way I can describe it is as a first instinct. Or maybe a still small voice whispering momentarily in my ear. But at that age, it was so brief and so faint, that I often wasn't sure if I'd heard it right. The good thing was that now I was paying attention and as far as I was concerned, it was God talking to me. As I got closer to God, that instinct got stronger. Countless times between the ages of eight and sixteen I would be asked a question in class and without knowing how, the right answer would pop up in my head. But then almost immediately I would think to myself, *are you sure?* And I'd fumble and my doubt would win. I would kick myself over and over again when I heard the right answer because I recognized it as the answer that I had originally heard in my thoughts.

I believe a lot of us can relate to this. So many times we make decisions against what we call our 'better judgement' and live to regret those decisions. Most of the time, what we call our 'better judgement' or 'gut feeling' or 'instincts' is actually the small voice of the Holy Spirit trying to talk to us and guide us.

Over the years and throughout my walk with God, it has become evidently clear to me that life would have been much easier if I had just learned to listen to my 'gut feeling.' Or better still, the voice of the Holy Spirit.

This truth was emphasized by Paul when he asked a very profound question of the Corinthians in the third chapter of his first letter to them. He said, "Don't you know that you yourselves are God's temple and that God's Spirit dwells in your midst?" The answer seems obvious to me now but at the time, I couldn't even conceive of the Holy Spirit, let alone think of Him as a constant companion to me. But that is what He is to each of us, a close personal friend who is always with us, teaching us, guiding us and giving us the right answers. In Akan, God is *Nyankopɔn*, which loosely translates into a friend upon whom if you lean, you are guaranteed never to fall. Admittedly, it's not easy to accept and trust a person you have never actually seen but over time, He proves Himself, if we give Him a chance.

The Spirit of truth. The world cannot accept him, because it neither sees him nor knows him. But you know him, for he lives with you and will be in you. John 14:17 (NIV)

THE SOVEREIGNTY OF GOD

For me, it was a few short years later that He proved Himself in a very profound albeit, scary way. I was somewhere between fourteen and fifteen years old, when the younger of my two older brothers, Kwafo, who was between sixteen and seventeen, was sent by my mother in her car on what was supposed to be an errand in the neighborhood. He could drive well. But since he wasn't yet eighteen, he didn't have a driver's licence and was forbidden by my parents from leaving the neighborhood. I was supposed to go on this errand with him, when I suddenly had an image in my head of my mother's car upside down, wheels still spinning and music playing.

When I saw this vision or image in my head, I paused momentarily as I rushed to get my slippers so that my brother wouldn't leave without me. But then, I wasn't quite sure whether it was God talking to me or just my imagination, so I ignored it. As I run back outside towards the car, my slipper tore. I bent over to examine it, when my brother, in a frustrated huff, drove off and left me at home. About an hour later, my parents received a frantic phone call from a stranger saying that my brother and his then girlfriend had been in a terrible accident.

Apparently, he had decided to leave the neighborhood to pick her up and take her on this errand. To make sure the detour did not make the journey time longer and arouse the suspicions of my parents, he was speeding and went round a bend too fast. The car somersaulted a couple of times and wound up on its back with the wheels up. Just like I had seen. He was fine. They both were.

Later that night, he told me that what struck him was that when everything had settled down, the music was still playing.

Again, just like I had seen.

I was so stunned by this revelation from my brother that I kept my vision to myself. I felt guilty and at the same time afraid. In fact, this is the first time I'm talking about it. It took the grace of God to preserve my brother's life and not leave me with the burden of knowing that I could have saved his life if I had just spoken up.

I was so haunted by this event that I spent weeks pondering over it and praying about it. I wondered what would have happened to me if my slipper hadn't torn. Certainly, I would have been in that car. I could have been dead by now! It reminded me of a student who died several years earlier when I was still at Ridge Church School. The poor kid was sitting against the wall in school, waiting to be picked up by his parents, when a car on its way to pick up another student lost control and squashed him against the wall. The next week, the school put up barriers to prevent that from ever happening again.

That incident haunted me for months and I could not understand why God allowed it to happen. As I pondered over it, I became even more puzzled. Why did God prevent some accidents and not others? As a priest, I still grapple with this question, especially when a young person dies. But whenever I have challenged Him on the death of anyone, He in turn asks me who I think should have died instead. My only consolation is that God in His sovereignty does not make mistakes.

> **I make known the end from the beginning, from ancient times, what is still to come. I say, 'My purpose will stand and I will do all that I please.' Isaiah 46:10 (NIV)**

WHEN FEAR SETS IN

We all have our stories of tragedy, adversity, lack and inadequacy and sometimes in our distress, we conclude that God has abandoned us. But God gains nothing from abandoning us and seeing us live in misery. On the contrary, God loves and adores us and has no desire to see us experience any kind of pain. He only wants us to come to the fullness of our joy by fulfilling the amazing plan that He has in store for us. But to get to that promised land, we must go through the wilderness.

This wilderness story has played itself out over and over again from Moses, to Joseph, to Daniel, to Jesus Himself. And yet when it comes to us, we somehow think we should be exempt. We hang on our cross and accuse God of forsaking us. But God has not forsaken us, not any more than He forsook Christ. He has simply set His plan in motion because as He told the prophet Jeremiah in Jeremiah 1:5 "Before I formed you in the womb I knew you, before you were born I set you apart; I appointed you as a prophet to the nations."

Nothing has changed since the days of Jeremiah. God has already orchestrated each of our lives and He knows exactly what He wants to do with us. But He has also given us free will and this free will is what the devil preys on. The devil plays with us by filling us with doubt and fear and the inability to properly discern. But we can rest assured that God is ever present in our lives. He never leaves us. He might be silent for a while...but He never leaves us.

One of the ways the devil sows seeds of discontent and disaffection in our lives is through fear. I have learned first-hand that fear is an extraordinarily powerful emotion but it is not necessarily an evil emotion. It only becomes evil when we mismanage it and do things to hurt ourselves and others. However, given that everything God created is perfect and fear is one of our emotions as human beings, it suffices to say that it has a useful purpose in our lives.

To begin with, fear is a self-preservation emotion. When I was pregnant with my daughter, I was cooking one day when I tried to lift the lid off a pot without protecting my hands. The steam from the stew burned my wrist and I dropped the lid. It crashed loudly to the ground and in the instant it hit the ground, my baby jumped in my womb. I had heard that babies can hear what happens outside the womb, but it had never struck me that an unborn baby would know enough to be frightened by a loud sound. Clearly, we are created with an instinct to respond to and move away from what we perceive to be dangerous situations.

We have an innate fear that is designed to keep us alive. But this same fear is the basis of many of the ungodly things we do as people. The fear of rejection can cause us to engage in fornication, because of peer pressure or because we believe everybody else is doing it. The fear of embarrassment can cause us to become timid and render us unable to explore our God-given abilities because we're afraid to make a mistake. Fear was my problem. Fear was my weakness. Especially, the fear of not being approved by others.

By the time I was fifteen, I was very sharp spiritually and could 'feel' very clearly from God. I can't say I ever 'heard' from Him. But I felt Him in my head and in my heart. I would have thoughts that were too intelligent to be mine. And I just knew it was God.

I remember, one day in Chemistry class at GIS, we were asked to explain why a very cold Coke freezes when it is opened. Without thinking, I knew it had to do with the inverse relationship between pressure and temperature. I was so sure of this, until another student suggested a different answer. Now this girl was a straight A-student. I, on the other hand, was a B-student on a good day. So I immediately deferred to her answer. The teacher went round the class and asked everyone to give their answer. No longer trusting my gut, I repeated her answer. Not only was I wrong, my original thought was right. I chose her answer over mine because I was afraid I'd be wrong and people would think I was dumb.

I had this constant fear within me. It made me feel on a daily basis that other people were better and more knowledgeable than I was. So, I constantly deferred to what they thought or said. This deference to other people's views and opinions plagued me into adulthood. It affected my confidence in myself and more tragically, it affected my confidence in God.

As I got older, my fear intensified to where I could no longer discern the voice of God. And my entire existence depended on other people's approval of me, especially young men. My grades slipped. Or more accurately, plummeted. I was performing so poorly in school that, I hit a new low where I failed my final exam and I was forced to repeat my second year in secondary school.

This failure and the ensuing embarrassment in front of my parents and classmates, was like a self-fulfilling prophecy. It only served to cement my already low self-esteem at the bottom of a deep dark pit. I could not feel the presence of God at all. The constant whisper of the Holy Spirit became faint. And then it disappeared.

In response, I decided academics were not for me. What was important was getting the approval of my mates. In other words, being 'cool'. Unfortunately, I just didn't have what it took. I didn't have cool clothes. Even if I did, I never had a great sense of fashion. I was a tomboy. All I ever wanted to wear was jeans and a t-shirt. I didn't realize that boys don't like girls who dress like them. So, even though I got along well with boys, they only wanted to be my friend. In fact, I became their go-to person when they were interested in a girl. Though this was not the attention I was looking for, it was some kind of attention, so I made it work for me.

What I found strange was that, though I wasn't popular with people my age, I was very well liked by adults. Several of my teachers became personal friends. They found me very sensible and wise and mature for my age. But at that time, I wasn't looking for their approval. I wanted to be a 'hot chick.' I wanted to be one of the girls that all the guys were after and yet everything I tried, failed.

I was a good athlete but that only made people think I was 'hard'. Not cute, or pretty or any of the things I wanted them to think. It didn't help that I struggled with eczema, which left my legs badly scarred. I felt miserable. And I blamed God. If He cared so much about me, how come He didn't make me cool? Why were my legs always somewhere between open bleeding sores and dark scars? Why did I struggle so much with basic Maths and Science principles?

Fear does that. It breeds in us a contempt for God. And it creates a gap between us and Him. For me, that gap made it impossible to hear God anymore. I was completely on my own and I stopped bothering to consult Him because I couldn't hear or feel anything anyway.

Sometimes, this gap between us and God can get so wide that in an effort to resolve our issues, we turn completely away from Him and towards the occult. Sometimes, we even allow our bodies to be violated by 'men of God' because our separation from God has left us feeling that it is these men who can solve our problems. Because it is in them and not in God that we have placed our hope. But whatever we turn to, as long as it is not God, the end result is the same. Our fears drive us to do things that are displeasing to God. For me, my constant fear of rejection, made me reject the person I had been created to be and to try to mold myself into the image of everyone else and not the image of God.

> **But the Lord God called to the man, "Where are you?"**
> **He answered, "I heard you in the garden and I was**
> **afraid...so I hid." Genesis 3:10 (NIV)**

We must remember that fear will come but when it does, we must manage it properly. Whether it is a fear of the unknown, or the fear of failure, or the fear of rejection, no matter how dark or scary a situation is, once we stretch out our hand to God, He will hold us and guide us through it.

Minnie Louise Haskins captures this succinctly in her poem 'The Gate of the Year' in which she wrote,

"I said to the man who stood at the gate of the year, 'Give me a light that I may tread safely into the unknown.' And he replied 'Go out into the darkness and put your hand into the Hand of God. That shall be to you better than light and safer than a known way.'"

The 'known way' for me was that my very existence and importance were anchored on the acceptance of my peers. Anything short of that meant I was failing. If only I had understood that my fear was unfounded and that all I needed to do was to stretch out my hand into God's hand, I would have saved myself a lot of pain and trouble. I would not have allowed fear to create in me such disdain for God.

Today, as a priest, I look back on those days and it is clear that I was not justified in my fears. I know now that God's plan for my life was already in motion and the approval or otherwise of my peers was never important to God. And yet there I was, so crippled by the fear of rejection, that any type of rejection was like an attack on my being. And I defended myself vehemently. This manifested very clearly when I was in Fifth Form.

The headmistress of GIS at the time called me into her office to ask me to drop out of my Science classes and take up only Art subjects, because she believed my grades would be an embarrassment to the school. Her rejection left me mortified. And angry.

So angry that I cried.

HOW ANGER DESTROYS

That's another emotion that can affect our relationship with God. Anger. I have found that anger numbs our senses to the voice and presence of God. But that's not all. Science has proven that anger damages us physically as well. There is a direct correlation between persistent anger and poor health. Conditions like high blood pressure, insomnia, depression, heart attack and skin problems, such as eczema have been linked to unmanaged anger. This is the real reason why God commands us to forgive others and let go of our anger. It is not so much about the person who has offended us, it is actually about us. Every day we go to bed angry at someone, we damage our own health and our anger has absolutely no impact, positive or negative, on the person with whom we are angry. In other words, it is a complete waste of time.

"In your anger, do not sin": Do not let the sun go down while you are still angry. Ephesians 4:26 (NIV)

But after being told that me and my grades were not good enough for GIS, heeding Ephesians 4:26, was not high on my priority list. That afternoon, I vowed in anger to make my headmistress sorry for all the things she had said to me. In my anger, I created a list I called the 'revenge list'. On this list were all the people I felt had offended me in one way or the other. My thinking at the time was rather unfortunate because in creating this revenge list, I robbed myself of the opportunity to communicate with God, the one person who has the ability and the desire to calm my angry heart.

It's important to note that the reason I didn't communicate with Him was that God was the first person on my revenge list! I know it sounds crazy but it's true. As a teenager, I was determined to take revenge on God. How ignorant and naïve! But that is what anger does...it blinds you and makes you irrational.

I held onto this vow for close to twenty years and what that meant was that I didn't talk to God. Not in any meaningful way. I was too busy planning my revenge against Him!

I was mad at Him because He had made me an uncool person. He hadn't made me smart, plus I had eczema which left me scarred. Also He hadn't given me the kind of body boys liked. And He had allowed one of our teachers to embarrass me in front of my entire class a few years earlier. The teacher in question was the second person on my revenge list.

This runner-up to God on my revenge list was a French teacher. I hated French! One day, we had an oral exam and we had to work through a telephone call in French. I was so nervous, that I forgot to ask as part of the exam who was on the phone. The next time we had French, she gave us our grades and of course I had failed. As a temperamental teenager, I challenged her and she called me a 'miserable cockroach' to the hearing of the whole class. The class burst out in laughter and needless to say, I was deeply embarrassed and angry. Very angry. That was how she made it onto the revenge list!

With a growing revenge list borne out of raw anger, it was only natural that when the headmistress called me into her office to essentially tell me that I wasn't good enough, she became the third person on my list. I expected her to be concerned about my welfare, not the reputation of the school. I was so upset I could barely stand still. I couldn't go home and tell my parents that my headmistress thought I was so dumb and that I was an embarrassment to the entire institution. So I wept on one of the teachers who had become my friend, Mr. Kyei, my Physics teacher.

He was furious about the situation and promised me that as long as I was committed, he would tutor me for free just to make a point to the headmistress. That was God intervening. But at the time, I didn't know. I was too preoccupied with what I believed would be the joy of revenge to pay attention to whatever God was doing.

Anger does that to us. It creates so much noise in our heads and blurs our eyes such that we cannot hear or see God despite His constant presence in our lives. All I knew was that, I had three months to convert my Cs and Ds to As and Bs in the London GCE O'Level examinations. And for that reason, every single day, Mr. Kyei and I worked together to prepare me for the exam.

At the end of that summer, when the results came out, my headmistress, without batting an eye or even questioning how, listed me as one of the students recommended for Science for Sixth Form. That made me even more furious. The fact that she didn't even notice the change in my grades left me peeved to no end.

Many of us are angry with people who don't even recognize they have offended us. So we let that anger eat us up and drive us crazy. I was so disappointed that my headmistress did not even notice she had hurt my feelings.

Admittedly, my anger towards her had driven me to succeed. I'm not by any means suggesting that anger should be our driver and motivator to do well in life, but it is worth noting that sometimes God uses what the devil intended to destroy us, to elevate us.

You intended to harm me, but God intended it for good. Genesis 50:20 (NIV)

But instead of this being a wake-up call for me, it only deepened my foolishness. I decided I would do well, amazingly well enough to go to university and pursue a Science degree. Because clearly this achievement of mine in secondary school had not impressed her sufficiently. This was the primary reason I chose Physics as a major in University and not something that I would have enjoyed more thoroughly and probably been better at. That is what anger does. It makes us expend energies that we could have used for something far more beneficial to us.

Refrain from anger and turn from wrath; do not fret - it leads only to evil. Psalm 37:8 (NIV)

After the episode with my headmistress, I vowed never to let anyone make me feel as though I couldn't have or accomplish anything. My attitude generally was good, at least to the extent that I began to take school more seriously. But the source of my attitude was poor. My motivation was pride. My anger had grown into unbridled pride, stemming from the fact that I was now doing well in school, despite what my headmistress had said.

THE PRIDE OF LIFE

During my last two years of secondary school, God often popped up in my head but for some reason, I never made the connection between Him and what was happening in my life. With the good grades for instance, I gave Mr. Kyei a lot of the credit but I still believed that ultimately it was I who had delivered the goods. I honestly did not think God had made any contribution. So I gave Him no credit. That was pride at its best. It made me feel that I was the author and creator of my recent success in school. As far as I was concerned, God had no part of it.

> **Be alert and of sober mind. Your enemy the devil prowls around like a roaring lion looking for someone to devour. 1 Peter 5:8 (NIV)**

In all our circumstances, especially our successes, the devil knows that God will not impose Himself on us. And so he quickly forces himself to the front of the line in the hope that we will get confused and think that we ourselves, or at best someone else but definitely not God, has delivered us. I fell fully for that trick and so instead of being gracious and grateful, pride and revenge became the hallmark of my life.

By this time, I had a long list of people on my 'revenge list.' People who teased me because of my scars. People who made me feel like I wasn't smart. People who wouldn't invite me to parties and hangouts because I wasn't cool enough. Even my brother, who sometimes made me feel like I was an embarrassment to him, was on my list! The list of people was endless and I had the time and energy for every single one of them!!

As the good Lord would have it, or maybe it was not the good Lord; either way, as fate would have it, when I started Sixth Form, I was old enough to drive and my parents gave me access to a really nice car to take to school. An Audi. Now I was cool. And to make me even cooler, my strong relationship with several teachers made it possible for me to park in the teachers parking lot even though it was strictly forbidden for students to park there. You can only imagine what that did to my already bloated pride. It made me prouder and my way of doing things became even more skewed.

PAIN AND BITTERNESS

Suddenly, people wanted to be my friend. Or so it seemed. But by this time I was beyond trying to fit in. I didn't want to fit in anymore. I wanted everyone who wanted to be my friend to know what it felt like to be rejected when you wanted in and no one would take you in. I was bitter and hurt. And I wanted everyone to feel it too. So I cut off everybody. I only made friends with and hang out with students who were obvious outcasts. As well as with a few other people who had been nice to me earlier. Those were the only people I allowed to ride in my Audi.

For the most part, I was a loner and I would often leave school during my free periods and go for a drive. I have always had a theme song for every activity and season of my life and in those days, my theme song was Tupac's 'Picture me rollin''. I would play it full blast on the stereo and yell the lyrics at the top of my voice, *"Picture me rollin' in my 500 Benz, I got no love for these ni***s, there's no need to be friends!"*

By this time, I had absolutely no relationship with God. I went to church with my mother because that was what I had always done. But God was not my friend. Strangely though, when I would go on these free-period drives, I would often drive to the Most Holy Trinity Cathedral on High Street. The Cathedral was nowhere near GIS. There were at least three other Anglican churches that were closer than the Cathedral. But my spirit was so drawn to it, that sitting in class, I would yearn for a free period so I could sneak off and go there and just sit.

The doors to the Cathedral were always open and there was never anyone in there. I knew no one would ever look for me there. I could revel in my aloneness and not have to worry about what the rest of the world thought. But I also went there because it was the one place I felt at total peace. I would always sit in the same pew at the back of the Cathedral, by the Western door and just be.

When I was there, time faded away. Pain faded away. And the whole world just disappeared. All that was left was the Cathedral and me. When I was there I never prayed. I just felt. It was such peace. Like I was home. Like I belonged. It was a safe place that didn't require coolness to qualify. I would sit for the entirety of my free time and then drag myself back to school. I remember those drives back to school were always so refreshing. I felt light and strong, almost like I was flying.

Twenty-three years later when I celebrated my first Mass as a priest in that same Cathedral, I knew without a doubt that God had never taken His hand off me. I now understood what Paul meant when he said, "He who has begun a good work in us will carry it on to completion." God, for over twenty years patiently watched me run through this maze called life. He watched me take so many wrong turns and even watched me take the same wrong turn multiple times. But He was never ever frustrated with me. He just allowed me on my own to come to a point of choosing Him and all the while, He shielded me from disaster.

> **I am with you and will watch over you wherever you go and I will bring you back to this land. I will not leave you until I have done what I have promised you. Genesis 28:15 (NIV)**

Many of us are still stuck in our wilderness loop. Like the people of Israel, we keep making the same mistakes over and over again. So what is supposed to be a three-day journey ends up taking the proverbial forty years. And that's if we are lucky. Most of us never make it out of the wilderness. But God derives no joy from our wilderness. He puts us in the wilderness, not for His pleasure but for our growth. Like Moses and John the Baptist, He needs us to break away from all the social hang-ups that slow us down. When we do that, then He can use us.

But I wasn't there. Not even close.

In a bid to draw attention to the fact that I was different, I joined the most 'outlandish' extracurricular club I could find. The Bible-Study club! Not because I loved or even cared about God. No. I joined for three reasons. The first was that I knew that GIS, as a secular school, had challenges with the club and I wanted that kind of controversy around me. Just so I could go against the grain. Secondly, because of its controversial nature, I knew it would have very few members, which meant I wouldn't have to deal with too many "annoying people." The last reason was that the teacher leading the club was a greatly feared Maths teacher. So again, I figured it was not likely to attract very many people.

When I look back, I can imagine that at the time, God must have been sad watching me choose Him, not because I loved Him but because I was angry, hurt and full of pride. But He also must have been deeply tickled knowing that I would wind up being one of His biggest advocates.

In my last year of secondary school, we all applied to universities outside of Ghana. I only applied to the universities that I was sure no one from my school was applying to. In fact, I had wanted to go to university in Ghana, because I knew everyone else was planning on going abroad. But the universities in Ghana were all on strike for various reasons so I had no choice but to look outside the country.

My brother was already in a University in the USA and my parents compelled me to apply there. And so I did. I also applied to a few other schools of my choosing. I was one of the first students to get accepted into any school. And when the news came out, many people congratulated me and said many positive things. But the only thing that stayed with me was a negative comment made by one student about how the university that had accepted me was not an Ivy League school and therefore, not a good school. I was so sad. And I used that statement to fuel my anger even more. I decided I was going to do something spectacular in university, just to make a point to everyone that, first of all, I wasn't dumb, and secondly, that I wasn't in a bad school. That anger, pride, pain and bitterness drove me. But they also pulled me away from God.

There are certain emotions and traits that when we entertain, prevent us from thriving. For me, it was fear, anger, pride and bitterness. For others, it can be addiction, envy, hate, vileness or even selfishness. These become barriers between us and God and it's critical that we work them out of our lives. I, by God's grace, managed to shed mine but I wasted so much of my life by allowing them to take control of my thinking.

The Bible already cautions against this and Paul best captures it in his letter to the Galatians where he says,

> **The acts of the flesh are obvious: sexual immorality, impurity and debauchery; idolatry and witchcraft; hatred, discord, jealousy, fits of rage, selfish ambition, dissensions, factions and envy; drunkenness, orgies and the like. I warn you, as I did before, that those who live like this will not inherit the kingdom of God. But the fruit of the Spirit is love, joy, peace, forbearance, goodness, faithfulness, gentleness and self-control. Against such things, there is no law.**
> **Galatians 5: 19-23 (NIV)**

I don't think I had ever even seen this passage while I was in school. But even if I had, in my pride and ignorance, I would probably have dismissed it. That notwithstanding, secondary school eventually came to an end and I graduated. Angry, bitter and hurt.

But also in love...

CHAPTER TWO

UNKNOWN DARKNESS

**The light shines in the darkness and the darkness did
not comprehend it.
John 1:5 (NKJV)**

...in love with Joseph.

Somewhere in the midst of all the foolishness of my secondary
school life, I met a young man called Joseph. We were both
sixteen years old then. He went to a different school and we
met at a mutual friend's house. I fell in love with him the moment
I saw him. He was the gentlest, sweetest person I had ever met.
And he was absolutely gorgeous. He wasn't like the other hunks I
knew in my school who were preoccupied with being hunks. He
was very polite and sensitive. A true gentleman. And he and I hit
it off like a house on fire. Every day he'd come over and we'd sit
outside my gate and watch cars drive by whilst we talked. We'd
talk for hours and we'd see each other off several times. In those
days my parents lived in Roman Ridge, on Onyasia Crescent. I'd
walk him up the street and he'd walk me back down to my gate.
Eventually we'd agree on a middle place where we could part. He
was one of the few people who made me feel alright with myself.
And it felt really good.

I didn't have to pretend with him. And I think it made him happy that I genuinely liked him for who he was and not just because he was exceptionally handsome. We started dating and my world with him was completely separate from my unhappy secondary school world.

About two years into this dating relationship, his entire family relocated to the USA. And just like that, he was gone. I was devastated. And even though I knew I would eventually go to the USA as well, it's such a big place. There was no guarantee I'd wind up in Houston where he was. And so just like that, he and all his wonderful specialness left me in Ghana. And with that, I reverted to looking for people who would make me feel cool before I left for university.

I found some. And that last summer before university was one big party. The world would call it a heck of a good time but honestly, it was a time when I was living in an unknown bondage. I say unknown, because I really didn't know I was in a bondage. I knew something wasn't right. I missed Joseph and I felt empty and wanted to be filled. But I didn't know what to be filled with, so I decided to fill it with 'fun'.

That year my father had been loaned to the Gambian Government for a few years as a judge and my mother had gone off to visit him for the summer. So at nineteen I found myself with three cars, cash and signed blank cheques. The only person to oversee me was my eighty-five year-old grandmother, who was... well...eighty-five!

So essentially, I had all the freedom a nineteen-year-old could ask for and two clear months within which all I needed to do was stay alive and get on a flight to the USA for university.

This largesse my parents had left for me, I suppose, would have made any teenager feel very content and happy. But not me. It did not fill the emptiness I felt. The truth is, at the time nothing could have made me content. I was too preoccupied with my inadequacies.

LIVING IN DENIAL

On hindsight, this freedom could have ruined my life. I know quite a few young people who have crumbled and even died under the burden of the kind of freedom that comes after secondary school. My only saving grace was that at nineteen, I had a good sense of responsibility.

Although I lived alone and could do anything I wanted, the fear of what my parents would do to me if I messed up, kept me in line. I didn't even consider being foolish with their money. But I was still a deeply insecure girl, in desperate need of approval from her friends.

In those days, having access to a car got you massive approval. So I was going to ride it for all it was worth. Several boys 'chased' me, or maybe it was the Audi I drove they were 'chasing'! It's hard to tell now. But either way, it made me feel beautiful and cool. So with the perfectly brewed blend of insecurity and the need for approval, the devil intervened in grand style and led me through a summer of clubbing and drinking.

I hated all of it! Well not the dancing. I still love to dance!

But I hated the rest of it. We spent countless nights in smoky and sweaty night clubs. I remember how the ash from all the smoke would settle on our clothes and in the strobe lights they would glisten. I thought that looked pretty! Everyone was covered in ash and everyone smelled like a cigarette butt. It was absolutely disgusting. But it was cool, so I sucked it up and went along.

My rationale was that, being cool had a price and that price was loneliness and sadness. And smelling bad. On countless occasions, I'd be sitting at a bar of one nightclub, or another, surrounded by my happy and laughing "friends" and in the middle of it all, I could literally feel myself leave my body and hover over the club watching me. I looked so happy with my drink and all the activity around me. But I felt so sad and lonely and drained. I was sad because I hated the taste of alcohol and yet I wasn't bold enough to just say no. I was lonely because I knew I didn't have a genuine friend in that crowd.

I could never understand why I always felt drained and mentally fatigued. It would be twenty years later that my counselor, Sika, would reveal to me that introverts feel drained by excessive external stimulation, whilst extroverts are energized by it. As a teenager, I thought introverts were smart, nerdy people. Definitely not cool people. Imagine my surprise to find that for years I had just been fighting against my God given introverted nature.

I'm not sure if it was the name of the club or just the fact that it jammed on Friday. Either way, every Friday we went to a club called Fridays. I was there so often that, the bouncer nicknamed me Ms. Friday. I thought that was very cool! It was some kind of approval. So I took pride in it. My thinking was that I was so cool, that even the bouncer knew who I was. It sounds mad to me now, because it was. Further proof that when we don't know who we are in Christ, the foolishness of men seems like wisdom.

My people are fools; they do not know me. They are senseless children; they have no understanding. They are skilled in doing evil; they know not how to do good. Jeremiah 4:22 (NIV)

Then on Saturday we would go to the Labadi beach party. There, we danced till the sun came up. A group called Nonchalant had come out with a hit which had a chorus that went like this, *"Five o'clock in the morning. Where you gonna be? Outside on the corner. You better get yourself together. While you're wasting all your time, right along with your mind."* Today, I would have immediately recognized the voice of God cautioning me through that song. But back then it was a heck of a song. And whenever it was played, I would be in the thick of the dance floor yelling the chorus at the top of my lungs and checking the time to make sure it was indeed five O'clock in the morning to further legitimize the song and my existence. And of course my coolness.

But despite this, all I felt was loneliness. I felt like I was dying inside. But I could never figure out what exactly was killing me. Was it because I myself didn't approve of what I was doing? What was strange for me was that, it didn't matter how much approval I got from the people around me, it just wasn't enough.

At dawn, I would drive myself home. I enjoyed those drives home alone. I loved watching the sun rise. And in those moments it was just me and my music and my real thoughts. Those drives were a time when I could be unapologetically me. I could speak to myself out loud and be truthful in my utterances. I had become my own best friend, my own closest friend. And when I spoke out loud, I heard a response in my head. It was always the response of someone who truly loved me and cared about me. Someone who would advise me to try and be happy without all the external approval. Listening to those thoughts always felt so peaceful and reassuring. Now I know it was God, being a friend to me.

But then I'd get home and the guilt would hit. Especially when I'd try and open the gate quickly and quietly for fear that some neighbor going for an early morning walk would see me and start giving me grief for being out till morning. Honestly, I don't think the issue was that I'd gone partying. I don't believe God has or had a problem with me going out. I think my guilt revolved around my intent. God knew and I knew that I didn't want to go partying. I only went out to be cool. To get approval. I was like a drug addict, who feels low and guilty when the highs come down and they are sober. So they do it again to take away the shame. But in the end they only wind up in a vicious cycle of addiction. I was not being true to myself. The Spirit of God rebelled against that dishonesty in me. And I wound up hating myself. I was too blind to see that neither cool cars, nor cool clothes, nor night clubs, nor alcohol, could define who I was in Christ.

DEALING WITH SELF-HATE

After all the unhappiness of secondary school, I was looking forward to university. I believed it would be a good opportunity for me to leave the old me behind. My hope was that, all the things I thought were wrong with me in secondary school would somehow be fixed in university. I hoped that this time, I would fit in and be cool. I hoped I would be light skinned enough. I hoped I would be voluptuous enough. I hoped I would be pretty enough. I hoped my world would be rich enough. I figured that if all these inadequacies and insecurities were out of the way, I would perform well in school and generally enjoy university.

But I was dead wrong. What I called 'inadequacies' in my life, were actually not inadequacies at all. God made me the way I was for a reason and I should have basked in it. Instead, I chose to view as negative everything that made me unique. Many of us struggle with this. We are so preoccupied with trying to be carbon copy of what we admire, that we fail to see anything admirable in ourselves.

We feel we are inadequate because we are not married, or

because we do not own a car, or because we are not very bright in school, or because we don't have a child. The list is endless. But these things that we call inadequacies are like tiny black spots on a large white cloth. We completely disregard the massive white areas, and all we focus on are the spots. The white sheet is our life, which is full of all the positive things that we have going for us. We really should be content with what we have and who we are. We should strive to be better people and not wallow in self-pity and self-hate.

I wish now that I had focused on all the positive things that were happening in my life then. I really do, because if I had, I would not have wasted so many years wallowing in the darkness of self-hatred and unforgiveness.

I call it 'darkness' because that blend of fear, anger, pride and lack of self-confidence prevented me from reflecting the light of Christ. I felt dark within me. My mind was dark and I projected that darkness onto many people, in some of the hateful things I said and did to them. That, I regret.

FINDING FORGIVENESS

One of the reasons why I was particularly glad secondary school had ended was because I thought it afforded me the opportunity to move away from a painful experience. Two years before secondary school was over, I was deeply betrayed by someone who for the last six years, had been one of my very best friends, Brian. He was an exceptionally brilliant young man. Topped every subject and was well liked by most people. For some reason he liked me. Now let me put things in perspective. As I have made abundantly clear, I had all along in secondary school longed for a sense of acceptance and belonging. So a brilliant and popular student like Brian taking a liking to me was a big deal.

We went everywhere together in school. Over the weekends, he would visit me so we could continue hanging out. We shared all kinds of secrets, including who we were interested in. He confided in me about his girlfriend and I did same about Joseph. At that age, we were all experimenting with each other and every new experience was scandalous and juicy. I held his information in confidence.

One day, out of the blue, he stopped taking my calls and started giving me the cold shoulder at school. It was very puzzling and very painful, because I had so few true friends, that my relationship with him was one that I held close to my heart. I did everything to try and figure out what I had done wrong. I even apologized unreservedly for anything I had done wrong ever since we were fourteen, which is when we met. But all of this fell on deaf ears. Neither he nor anyone else would tell me what I had done to cause me to lose my close friend. I cried over this for many weeks and I talked to a mutual friend, Rasheed about it. He advised me to forget about Brian. So I did. I spent months steeling my heart against him and against allowing anyone to ever get that close to me again.

Several months later, Rasheed asked me if Brian and I had resolved our issue. I still had no idea what the said issue was so I just said, "no." It was then that he explained to me that all along, Brian had been led to believe by another young man that I had betrayed his trust and shared a secret that he (Brian) had told me. Apparently, Rasheed had tried to explain to Brian that there was no way I would do that but he was so hurt by what he believed was true, that he decided to cut me off. But now there was a new development, which was why Rasheed had brought up the issue. Brian now had new information, which cleared my name but he wasn't quite sure how to approach me after what had been close to a year of ignoring me. So he asked Rasheed to apologize to me on his behalf and try to reconcile our friendship.

What I felt, as Rasheed spoke was a mixture of relief and hate. Relief that I now knew what had destroyed my relationship with Brian. But hatred at Brian for not trusting me to begin with, I could not understand how his trust in me could be so easily shaken. I knew if the situation were reversed, there was no way I would have doubted him especially on the word of the person who had told him this tale about me. It was a chap called Sebastian, whom I had always viewed as a rascal. This led me into a downward spiral of deep hatred. I hated Sebastian for lying about me to Brian. I hated Rasheed for waiting all this time to tell me the truth. And of course, I hated Brian for not trusting me and ruining a friendship that I valued so much. This hatred and my inability to forgive them, only exacerbated the darkness swirling in my life.

> **But anyone who hates another brother or sister is still living and walking in darkness. Such a person does not know the way to go, having been blinded by the darkness. 1 John 2:11 (NIV)**

I told Rasheed I wanted to hear from Brian himself. I wanted to hear him apologize personally. He eventually came over to my home and we talked for a long time. He apologized profusely and I accepted his apology but I could not forgive him. I could not forgive any of them. And he knew it. Things were never the same between us. One day, one of our teachers called me into her office after school. She asked what had happened between Brian and me. I just said we had a small misunderstanding. She then handed me an essay written by Brian as part of his application to university.

In answering the question, "Describe a time in your life when you made a mistake that you regret?" He wrote an essay about our falling out. I wept when I read that essay but somehow for me, the damage was done and I could never forgive him. That inability to forgive Brian, was a grave mistake. And it fed other negative traits.

> **Get rid of all bitterness, rage and anger, brawling and slander, along with every form of malice. Be kind to one another, tenderhearted, forgiving one another, as God in Christ forgave you. Ephesians 4:31-32 (NIV)**

I started training my mind to dislike and mistrust everyone. I developed a very cold attitude towards people, telling myself over and over again that I neither liked nor cared for anyone. But what I was doing was actually sinking into depression and self-hate. This self-hatred fueled the things I did that summer. Everyone I talked to, hang out with, drank with, in my mind was a person I was using to get ahead in my quest for coolness. But deep inside me, I was sad. Very sad. I wish I had forgiven my friends for hurting me and forgiven myself for harboring such hate. The nature of God is such that it is impossible to harbor hate and unforgiveness and still be happy. The only way we can truly overcome the kind of sadness and depression I experienced, is to forgive others and rid ourselves of all bitterness.

To refuse to do so is to sin. Since God forgives us, we honestly have no right to hold grudges or seek revenge against anyone. Not only does our unforgiving, vengeful, or bitter spirit affect the people around us, it separates us from the blessings of God. The bottom-line is we must forgive others no matter what the offense.

> Then the master called the servant in. "You wicked servant," he said, "I canceled all that debt of yours because you begged me to. Shouldn't you have had mercy on your fellow servant just as I had on you?" In anger his master handed him over to the jailers to be tortured, until he should pay back all he owed. "This is how my heavenly Father will treat each of you unless you forgive your brother or sister from your heart." Matthew 18:32-35 (NIV)

I have come to recognize that the sadness I felt was really the conflict between my spirit and the Holy Spirit. But as much as I sinned and deliberately turned my back on God and on myself, God simply would not let go of me. It didn't matter what I did, my conscience was never seared. This guilt from God or better said, this piercing of my conscience by God hounded me for years. If only I had forgiven Rasheed, Brian and Sebastian, I would have done myself a lot of good and perhaps, insulated myself from the hell I found myself in later in life.

GOD'S GUIDANCE EVEN WHEN WE CAN'T FEEL HIM

In those day, I did nothing on Sundays. I was not a church goer because I found church boring and irrelevant. I found Christians hypocritical and unkind and I didn't want to be around them. I felt the church didn't accurately represent the God I felt within me, certainly not the God who answered my prayer when I was eight.

My parents were not particularly religious then, as per the definition of most people. My mum went to church every Sunday and my Dad went occasionally. My father was Presbyterian, and although a son of a Presbyterian priest, I suspect he was just fed-up with church. My mother is an Anglican, and as children we were permitted to go to Sunday school at either denomination.

I liked the Anglican Church, because the service was short and I loved the orderliness and the solemnity of the Mass. It made me feel in touch with God. I loved it when the priest sang the prefaces and the whole church sang the Lord's prayer during the consecration of the bread and wine for communion. That chanting and singing did something for my soul. Something which boys and clubs and drinks and even dancing could not do. It filled me up. But it was so short and it was just once a week. It never crossed my mind that I could have had that feeling every day of my life if I wanted. I think that even though I was not at a good place emotionally and psychologically, God used those short bright moments of communion in church to remind me of His ever present light and guidance. That is, when I attended church.

Looking back, my life at that time reminds me of a popular poem called "Footprints in the Sand". It speaks to how the author was walking with God and she could see both her footprints and God's footprints at the beginning of the walk. And yet in her time of greatest distress, she could see only one set of footprints. The author assumed God had abandoned her, but discovered later that God had actually been carrying her. I've always associated this poem with a person who knew God and had given their life to Christ and felt abandoned later in the journey. But I think the real beauty of this poem is that it also speaks about those who don't know God at all and yet all the time He walks with us and sometimes carries us.

These are the times when the devil can easily snatch our lives away from us, or mess us up forever. But that is why God carries us, because He knows how vulnerable we are. He carries us despite the fact that we don't acknowledge Him. He carries us despite the fact that we laugh at Him. He carries us despite how we may belittle Him. I look back now and remember the countless arguments I had with people who tried to talk God with me. I would spit fire at them because God in my view was not consistent and His Church was made up of hypocrites. But as imprudent as I was, God continued to reach out to me, hoping that like the prodigal son, I would one day come to my senses and head back home to Him.

> **But God demonstrates his own love for us in this: While we were still sinners, Christ died for us. Romans 5:8 (NIV)**

I suppose that is why despite the fact that we weren't allowed to leave school unannounced, I could run off on my Cathedral drives and never got caught. I don't recall ever being worried that I'd be caught. I actually used to drive out of the school gates and not once did the guards or any teacher ask where I was going. It was as though they couldn't even see me. I believe that was God breaking protocol for me, so we could spend some quality time together.

Any rational thinking person would have seen that the church is where my heart and my love were but it honestly never occurred to me, because the church was not where 'coolness' was. I didn't know one cool person who went to church on their own volition. It didn't even come up. GIS just wasn't that kind of school. We were an International School. We focused on understanding each other. And religion was not part of that understanding. Hence, religions' position as a volunteer after-school program, in the form of the Bible Study club.

One afternoon, during a club meeting, one of my close friends, David, who was also part of this Bible club, said to me that, given my contributions to the discussions, he thought one day, I would become a priest. I was so angered by his comment that, we got into a fight about it. David and I had been friends for about two years by then. This was how we became friends:

There was a school election for head-girl and head-boy. I ran for head-girl against Brian's girlfriend. Although we were still friends at this point, Brian obviously wasn't going to help me and I understood that. But I felt rather alone, because he was the person with whom I would have thought through my campaign. About two weeks into my campaign, David, who was very quiet and withdrawn and definitely uncool, maybe even as uncool as me, walked up to me and said nothing.

"Errrm yeah?" I asked. I was very defensive in those days.

"So, the thing is I don't like you but I like your opponent even less, so I'm going to help you." He said it bluntly and then walked away as if we had reached an agreement.

There was something I liked and respected about his approach. It was annoying but there was something very strong about it. I knew he couldn't win me the popular votes but his mind fascinated me and I chose that and his friendship over the election. I lost but I gained a true friend in David. Some twenty-two years after David said I would become a priest, I was ordained as the seventh female priest in the Anglican Diocese of Accra.

The day I was ordained as a priest, was the first day all of us as new priests served communion. Naturally all your friends and family want to be in line to eat communion from your hands, because there is such a fresh anointing on your life. As the only woman to be ordained that day, my line of communicants was very long and it was important for me to serve everyone as diligently as I could. As each person would approach, I would look into the ciborium to make sure I was picking a perfect wafer. And then I would look up at the person and serve them while saying the words, "Receive the body of Christ, the bread of heaven." After I had served a countless number of people, I looked up to serve the next person and there in-front of me, beaming from ear to ear stood David. He had flown in from the USA just for my ordination! I was so excited to see him, I almost jumped up to hug him. I smiled, blessed him and served him communion. After the ordination ceremony, he came to me and said, "Hey, do you remember, that when you were eighteen I predicted that you'd become a priest?"

"Yeah whatever." I said dismissively with a smile.

He giggled and said, "Maybe I should become a prophet."

How annoying!

For some reason, I never told anyone about my secondary school trips to the Cathedral until after I was ordained and was posted by the Bishop back to the same Cathedral as a priest. It was not until the day I celebrated my first Mass as a priest at the Cathedral, that the memories came flooding back to me. As I stood there singing the Mass, that I loved so much as a teenager, I looked back to the pew I sat on all those years ago and I could feel God's presence so strongly. It was as though He were smiling down on me and saying, "Now you are home!"

CHAPTER THREE

GROWN BUT NOT MATURE

Rescue the weak and needy; save them from the hand of the wicked. They do not know or understand; they wander in the darkness.
Psalm 82:4-5 (NIV)

BEAUTY IS AN ATTITUDE

September 1996 was the start of university. At the time, I believed I had transitioned into full adulthood and maturity. Adulthood, yes. Maturity, definitely not.

In the beginning, the academics of school were easy. Most of what we did, I had covered in my A-Levels and so for the first time, I was feeling like some kind of academic superstar. I remember one day my grade was taken out of the statistics of a Maths exam because it was so high it was considered an outlier. I wish I had stayed on that trajectory. But in my usual pattern of searching for other people's approval, I quickly determined that academic excellence was not the way to be cool in university. In fact, it only got me labeled as a nerd, so I quickly moved away from that to academic mediocrity so I could fit in better.

My brother as usual, and very much unlike me, was very cool. He had been at the university for two years before I came and in that time, he had landed himself this very pretty African-American girlfriend.

I figured that was also what I needed to do: Find myself a boyfriend. And make that my claim to fame. Except there was a problem. I was not cute, no boys chased me except the boys who chased every girl in sight. This was very painful for me. It was like secondary school all over again. The harsh reality hit, that the problem was not my secondary school or Ghana. The problem was me. I just wasn't attractive. I didn't look like the people on TV, or in the magazines. And I just needed to come to terms with it.

The true pity was that like so many young women still do today, I looked to magazines to tell me what true beauty was. Magazines tend only to focus on external beauty and good looks. None of us, whether we are men or women, should ever seek validation by using our physical appearance only. The world of fashion, cosmetics and glamour, may claim that our looks supersede all things, but the truth is, it is the Spirit that dwells within us that makes us who we are.

The Spirit gives life; the flesh counts for nothing. John 6:63 (NIV)

Without the right attitude, the most beautiful of us cannot sustain a job, or friendship, or marriage, or most importantly, a good relationship with God. In fact, a truly beautiful person is a person who is joyful, peaceful, patient, kind, gentle, faithful, is good to other people and has self-control. That certainly was not me. I was so focused on outer beauty that I spent no energy working on my attitude. And it showed.

Many of us, especially young women, get caught in this trap of thinking that our looks are our way up and out. And so we violate our bodies with sex, drugs and all kinds of vices in the name of getting ahead either academically, financially, or in my case for popularity.

But it is God and hard work that gets us good grades, money or whatever we want. Not men, some of whom, as unfortunate as it may be, are only interested in enjoying themselves physically and leaving us with nothing but emptiness, shame and guilt.

Don't get me wrong. There is nothing wrong with physical beauty. It should be celebrated. But that celebration should be, within the integrity of studying for good grades, within the discipline of working hard for money and within the confines of marriage. Outside of these confines, we glorify ourselves and not God.

> **Your beauty should not come from outward adornment, such as elaborate hairstyles and the wearing of gold jewelry or fine clothes. Rather, it should be that of your inner self, the unfading beauty of a gentle and quiet spirit, which is of great worth in God's sight. 1 Peter 3:3-4 (NIV)**

BONDAGE UPON BONDAGE

Now, here I was in the USA feeling disillusioned, because contrary to what I had hoped, I was still uncool. I felt dumb because my grades were genuinely suffering now. I felt miserable. I was homesick, I was lonely and I even though my parents were paying for my tuition, I myself was broke.

This was the state I was in when I met Evelyn. She was a second year student. She and I decided to move off campus and share an apartment in order to save money. That was when the real nightmare of my university days began. Evelyn introduced me to clubbing and drinking in a way that I had never seen before.

All her friends were white, including her boyfriend. And they convinced me that in the USA, university was all about drugs and alcohol. So weekend after weekend, we would party, with the sole aim of getting drunk.

Whenever I'd say I didn't like the taste of alcohol, she and her boyfriend would literally fall on the floor laughing. I hated that they laughed at me, so I convinced myself that I liked the taste of alcohol, just to get their approval.

And so I drank and clubbed. I kept telling myself over and over again that this was 'the life.' It had to be, because at last I fitted in with a group of people and nobody was teasing me. The truth is, I hated it but everyone else seemed to be loving it. So I tried to learn to love it too. What I didn't know then was that, when you know who you are in Christ, you don't make excuses for not getting involved in things you don't want to do. You just say no!

As I danced in night clubs I felt empty. It didn't matter which clubs we went to, or how cute all the guys told me I was, I felt empty. And I had this persistent guilt. It was as if the Holy Spirit just wouldn't leave me alone. I had a constant battle within me.

Over time, my world and interestingly my clothes darkened. I came to a point where I only bought and wore black or dark clothes. I was depressed. I looked terrible. I had lost so much weight and yet was obsessed with being "skinny" because that was what the magazines said was attractive. I knew I needed to get away, and that's when God intervened in the person of Howard Blanning. Howard was a professor at my university whom I had met in Ghana the year before I started university. He had brought a number of students, including my brother, to Ghana that summer. And my parents hosted them a few times. Howard had a house which he allowed foreign students to live in for free. The only condition was that the house needed to be kept clean. I spoke to him and within a few weeks I moved into my room in his attic. I loved it. It was tiny but very well put together. And it was mine. I could stay there, enjoy my own company, and never had to feel the Evelyn pressure to go out and party.

> **He reached down from on high and took hold of me.**
> **Psalm 18:16 (NIV)**

ALAS! SOME GOOD NEWS

One day the phone in Howard's house rang and one of my housemates, a Czech guy, yelled up to me that the call was mine. I only got calls from my parents, so I came down expecting to speak to either my mum or my dad.

"Hello!"

"Hi Akua, this is Joseph." *Joseph!?* I was amazed. I hadn't heard from him in at least a year. He said he wanted to give our relationship a chance. So much of a chance that he had decided to move to my university to be with me. He wanted to transfer schools and relocate. It was like a miracle!

His leaving Ghana had left me truly sad and left a large gaping hole in my heart and in my life for that matter. I had gotten into such negative behavior and even though I had not heard from him since then, his sudden reappearance onto the scene was like a dream come true. Or so I thought!

I felt he would come and fill that hole in my heart. I suddenly felt as if God was finally pulling in my direction. In my typical dependency style, I started to envision how his presence and our relationship would make me cool and therefore happy. I had no idea that it would just be a continuation of the darkening of my mind and a deepening of my fears and insecurities.

In life, it is important to recognize that, the devil will sometimes use the most wonderful people in our lives as a weapon against us. When Peter scolded Jesus for saying He would die, Jesus said, "Get behind me Satan." He didn't chastise Peter because He knew it had nothing at all to do with Peter. It was all about the evil spirit behind Peter's utterance. Peter himself had the cleanest of intentions but the devil had other plans.

IT WAS NOT GOOD NEWS AFTER ALL

Within a few months, Joseph moved. I felt that now I could show all these university kids that I had been cool for a long time. My identity became tied up in who he was. He was how I introduced myself. I was his girlfriend. He had become my reason to be accepted and acceptable. And I believed that being with him should have given me honor in the eyes of all. We decided to move in together in an effort to make our relationship work better. But the exposure to his everyday life and how many women pursued him became a deep source of insecurity and misery for me.

I lived in constant fear of losing him. Fear that the scales would one day fall off his eyes and he would realize I'm completely uncool and go and find himself a worthy woman. This thought plagued me and had me on tenterhooks for the entirety of our relationship. I became excessively needy and clingy. And it burdened Joseph. He became emotionally distant and the more he distanced himself, the more afraid I became and the more I held on.

In the end, my redemption and my savior, the one who I expected to bring calm to the turbulence in my life, rather became a source of perpetual anxiety. Proof that, true redemption is found in God alone and not in any human being.

THERE ARE NO BOUNDARIES TO GOD'S FAITHFULNESS

Joseph had always been religious and when we were teenagers, I would always tease him about it. He was far less religious in university but we both knew to turn to God when we were 'broke'. Which was all the time. So we prayed a lot. I knew living together like we were was wrong but at that stage in my life, the coolest thing I'd ever done was to be dating and living with this total stud. But God remained faithful.

One day, I was going through our bills or as we called them at the time, "hate mail" when I realized that our cable bill was due the next day. We had absolutely no money in either of our bank accounts but I was due to be paid in two days' time. So we did the math and figured that if we paid the bill by cheque, it would take three days to clear. But it would be counted paid on the day we presented the cheque. I knew my salary would hit my bank account before the cheque cleared and we would be fine. As a broke student, this kind of maneuvering was quite routine and I wasn't particularly worried. That is until I went to work that night and was told that for some reason, I would not be paid for another week.

I completely freaked out. All of a sudden, my cable bill had gone from $32 to $102 because not only would the cheque bounce and draw a $35 bounced cheque fee, the cable company would charge a late fee of $32. Meanwhile, my total salary expectation for that week was $152. This was not good.

I told Joseph that we needed to pray for God to send us some extra money to cover this bill. So we prayed. We had Thursday, Friday, Saturday, Sunday and Monday to pray. The cable company late fee letter would be in the mail by Tuesday. So we prayed. A lot. But nothing happened. No one brought any money. Nothing happened at all.

I felt extremely disappointed in God, so much so that Joseph and I never discussed it. We just waited in gloom for the letter from the cable company. Then on Tuesday, the letter showed up in the mail.

We knew it was the late fee notice and we were so sad that we just left it on the dining table overnight without even opening it. Finally, the next evening, we decided to open it, resigned to the fact that we had to donate almost my entire salary to this 'one' bill. So I opened it. But there was no letter. What we found was a hand written post-it note that read, "Dear customer, we accidentally tore your cheque while we were opening your envelope. Please send us another cheque. There will be no late fee." The note was clipped to my cheque which had been ripped right through the middle.

Joseph and I stood in stunned silence. My hands shook as I held up the note to him. We were both so frightened that we threw the post-it note and the ripped cheque away like they were something evil and we never spoke about it again until just a few years ago.

> **Because of the Lord's great love we are not consumed, for his compassions never fail. They are new every morning; great is your faithfulness. Lamentations 3:22-23 (NIV)**

I regret now that we didn't frame that cheque. It was a miracle from God and we should have used it as a testimony to God. Again, it spoke to the depth of my lack of faith and my ignorance about God and what He is capable of. Rather than celebrate, we hid. I was ashamed that if I told people, I'd be accused of being too 'God-fearing'.

I feel very bizarre writing this now, but that was how I felt. I was so preoccupied with being cool and accepted by people that, it never once crossed my mind that I could be cool in Christ. Later in life, this situation made me see that we limit God when we tell Him how to solve our problems. It never crossed my mind to ask God to let anything happen to the cheque. In my mind, the only solution was for me to get some additional money. God was faithful to me, despite all my iniquities.

It's difficult to understand why God would be so good to me when my whole life was drowning in sin. But that attribute of God in itself is a demonstration of how beautiful He really is. God does not demand or even expect perfection from us. If He thought for a second that we could measure up or even come close to His holy standards, He wouldn't have allowed Christ to die for us. He knows there is a gap between us and Him because of our sinful nature and this is what creates this constant tension within us. That's what creates the guilty discomfort in us. But many of us instead of asking God to help us clean up our act, do one of two things. Either we try to lower God's standards, or we try and live a life of perfection.

Neither one of these works!

All God wants from us is to place our faith in Jesus, receive Him into our lives and He will take care of the rest. He will forgive us and as the Psalmist says, "lead us down the path of righteousness."

GOD ORDERS OUR STEPS

During the summer vacation between my third and final years of university, I couldn't afford to go home, so I applied for and received funding from some big company to run some electromagnetic experiments using equipment they had provided to the university's Physics department. A few weeks into this research job, I discovered there was something wrong with the equipment. I spent the rest of my summer trying to fix the equipment. And I loved it. I loved working with my hands and running all these sequential tests trying to eliminate faults.

That was how I discovered my love for working on machines. I didn't know what that was called, but I had the wherewithal to discuss it with my research advisor. He told me it was called Mechanical Engineering. Not only that but there was an entire department dedicated to teaching Mechanical Engineering. All those students in that department, for four years, got to have fun working on machines and come out on the other end with a degree. It was the most exhilarating feeling, to discover that I could study in a field I loved. That I could actually enjoy school.

I felt like I had been wasting my life doing Physics. I wanted to switch majors but with one year to go, I decided it would be better to finish the degree and then apply for a master's degree in Mechanical Engineering. Maybe if I had understood that the words of my secondary school headmistress, were not her words at all but actually God trying to order my steps, I would not have selected Physics as major in university with the intention of proving her wrong for the sake of my pride. I would have had the temerity of heart to listen to God and by so doing, save myself the heart ache of studying a course I did not thoroughly enjoy. Maybe I should have listened to my parents when they told me I could study anything I liked. And not been so preoccupied with my headmistress and her opinion of me.

That last year of university, I applied to graduate school to pursue a master's degree in Mechanical Engineering. I knew my parents couldn't afford to pay for it and I didn't have much money, so I was forced to defer for a year and work a job for the fees. The plan was to work, save and then go back to school.

Once again, I turned to my 'emergencies-only' God and prayed that He should help me find a good job. I wasn't willing to leave Joseph again, so part of the prayer was that the job needed to be close by. Almost immediately, God came through. I can still see it. I was walking by a notice board in school with hundreds of jobs posted on top of each other all over the board. This was a notice board I had walked past hundreds of times in the four years I'd been in university. But that day, I felt that small voice from my secondary school days suggest that I look for a job there. So I did. I stopped, glanced rather pessimistically at the jobs when suddenly, a particular job posting jumped out at me.

It was a one-year internship to work as a Chemical Engineer with the Procter & Gamble company (P&G). The obvious challenge was that; I didn't have a chemistry degree. The not so obvious one was that, I practically failed chemistry in university. Despite these two clear reasons why I should not apply for the job, 'something' told me the job was mine. The same thing that told me truths when I was eight, told me the job was mine. So, I applied for that job and I applied for nothing else. I was called in almost immediately for an interview. Not having a strong chemistry background, I was very concerned. But the interview turned out to be lunch with one guy who was more interested in my ability to pay attention and take diligent experimentation notes than anything else. The next month, I started with my new job at P&G.

That 'something' that told me to apply for the job despite the fact that I didn't have the right qualifications was the Holy Spirit. God was ordering my steps and preparing me for what was ahead, despite the chaos in my life.

> **Not that we are sufficient in ourselves to claim anything as coming from us but our sufficiency is from God. 2 Corinthians 3:5 (NIV)**

SECURITY IN GOD BREEDS SECURITY IN SELF

I liked my new job. Apart from the fact that it paid very well, it was a lot of fun. I had to carry out a series of experiments for some ground breaking research that P&G was doing. I relished the meticulous nature of the work and I felt a part of something important. The only down side was that the job was about a forty-minute ride from home and from Joseph.

Anytime I called and he didn't pick up, or wasn't where I expected him to be, I would panic. And with each day, my fear of him having an affair mounted. My fear was so severe that even though I could afford an apartment in the city close to where my job was, I chose to remain in the university town just so we could live together. Or more truthfully, so I could keep an eye on him. I had become so crippled by the notion of leaving him alone on campus that I opted to make the forty-minute ride each day.

I don't know why I thought then that my presence would make a difference. I believed if I was away for too long in a day, he would cheat on me. It got so bad that I would often sneak away from work, sometimes just to spend a few minutes with him and somehow keep him faithful. One day, I snuck away from work and half way to Joseph, it started to snow. A very powdery, slippery snow. 'Something' told me repeatedly to turn around and go back to work. But I just kept pressing on. Suddenly my car skidded off the road, hit a sign post and ran into a ditch.

I was completely helpless. I didn't know what to do. I couldn't get out of the ditch, I didn't have a phone and I hadn't asked for permission to leave the office. I was hoping a police car would come by, because I had assumed that would be my salvation. Then a car pulled over. A tall, slim, well-dressed middle-aged gentleman stepped out. He was handsome, had brown hair and was dressed in a suit and one of those shin length winter coats that you typically see on trendy Wall Street businessmen.

He was actually quite out of place for small-town America. But there he was walking towards my car with some urgency. He tapped on my window. I rolled it down and he said, "if the cops find you they will fine you for knocking down the signpost."

I had never heard such a thing before and I panicked. The last thing I needed was to get in trouble with the Police. He opened my door and said, "move over and let me get you out of the ditch." And with what appeared to be no effort, he maneuvered my car out of the ditch and then strangely parked it facing back to my office. He got out and with no more than the words, "be safe," he sat in his car and drove off. I believe he was an angel from God. But as usual, my fear of God's demonstrated power caused me to quietly drive back to the office and speak nothing of the incident to anyone.

Looking back, this incident seems to be a great metaphor for the state of my life at that point and what I needed to do to find redemption. The fact that I left the office without asking for permission could be equated to the things I did without consulting God. Heading to Joseph at a time I should have been at work symbolized the fact that my life was heading in the wrong direction. The ditch I drove into was a metaphor for the fact that since I was heading towards the wrong direction in life, I was bound to hit a bad patch. A wilderness if you will. The sudden appearance of a stranger represented God's readiness to come to our aid when we are in trouble. Finally, the fact that my good Samaritan pointed my car in the right direction, was emblematic of the fact that once we allow God to come into our lives and take us away from the snag we have encountered, He redirects us to the righteous path.

I wish I felt secure in God at that time. Had I been, I would not have found it necessary to keep an eye on Joseph for fear of being cheated on. I would just have trusted God to order my life as He saw fit.

> **For He will command His angels concerning you to guard you in all your ways. They will lift you up in their hands, so that you will not strike your foot against a stone. Psalm 91:11-12 (NIV)**

IT IS A SAD THING TO SEEK VALIDATION FROM THE WORLD

One day, I found a lump in my breast.

I was almost excited about it. In fact, if I'm being honest, I think I actually was, because it won me Joseph's full attention. He seemed a little less preoccupied with all the women paying attention to him and went with me on my various hospital visits. Eventually, it was determined the lump was probably not cancerous but needed to be removed because it would continue to grow and deform my breast. On the day of the surgery, Joseph took me in and when it was over, he brought me home.

That first night after the surgery was terrible for me. I reacted very badly to the pain medication and spent most of the night throwing up. Joseph had gone off to work and was due back by eight that evening. By midnight, he was not back. I had no way to reach him. I lay in bed, feeling high from pain medication and weak from the vomiting. Because I couldn't sleep, I heard him when he came in at four in the morning. Any rational woman would have been hurt and upset with him for abandoning her like that. I was hurt and upset. But not with him. I was upset with myself for not being enough to hold his attention. Over time my breast healed and the lump proved to be non-cancerous and everything went back to normal. Joseph was handsome and I was insecure.

Then it finally happened. He cheated on me.

My whole world crumbled. I went into a very dark place in my mind. A place I know I can't find my way back to now. I became deeply depressed. I wanted out of the relationship but I couldn't let go of him because he was my only source of self-worth. He justified my being and my inclusion. In as much as Joseph leaned on me in so many ways, I never saw those things as strengths. All I saw was that I wasn't pretty and certainly not pretty enough for this super handsome man.

Joseph tried to help by telling me over and over how beautiful and smart I was. He constantly said that I had no reason to feel insecure around any woman because I was amazing. But my brain kept telling me that actions speak louder than words. Every time he glanced at another woman, or complimented one, or found one attractive, my brain would tell me that it was because I wasn't good enough for him. His cheating was the victory my mind needed, to prove once and for all that Joseph was looking for someone better because I wasn't worthy. Him cheating was therefore proof that my mind was right.

> **For our struggle is not against flesh and blood but against the rulers, against the authorities, against the powers of this dark world and against the spiritual forces of evil in the heavenly realms. Ephesians 6:12 (NIV)**

I was devastated. My heart physically hurt. I so desperately wanted him to beg me for forgiveness and reassure me. He did. But somehow nothing he did or said was enough for me. For months, all I wanted to talk about was the affair. It wore both of us out but in as much as we talked, I couldn't find any healing. Over time, my pain turned to anger and I used that anger to fuel my work. That year, I published two scientific papers but still I didn't feel worthy.

I started going to church to see if I could find healing. I tried utilizing Buddhist meditative practices and read all kinds of self-help books. But I continued to struggle. Everyday got darker and darker. His affair was a self-fulfilling prophecy. It confirmed for me that I was unattractive and unworthy of love from any man. It consumed me. It was like a rain cloud that constantly followed me. Raining on me and darkening my world. The darkness in my brain became so intense that I decided to seek professional help.

That decision took a lot of courage, because I grew up in a world where only crazy people sought help for mental health issues. I was so ashamed of it that I kept it a secret, especially from Joseph. I saw my therapist twice a week and all I would do was cry. I felt so low and insignificant in every aspect of my life. She quickly recognized and pointed out to me one day that despite my education and my job and being accepted into graduate school to continue my education, the only thing that I felt gave my life value was my relationship with Joseph. To make things worse, because I was so sure I was unattractive and certainly not attractive enough to be with him, I had indeed become ugly.

I weighed less than a hundred pounds, my skin looked terrible and I only wore very dark and dowdy clothes. Seeing myself through her eyes startled me. When I got home that evening and opened up my wardrobe I discovered that the brightest item of clothing I had was a wine sweater. Everything else was black, dark grey or dark brown. I had not noticed but over the years, I had taken to buying darker and darker clothes. She told me that because I believed I was not pretty, I made no effort to look pretty. I barely smiled. In fact, I had a constant frown and I sounded agitated and condescending when I spoke.

As I continued to see her, it became apparent that there had always been a void within me dying to be filled. I had filled it with Joseph and made him responsible for my happiness. Not only was that an impossible task, it was an unfair task. So when he couldn't fill my heart, I blamed myself and that further deepened that void.

Through her sessions, I accepted that I needed to find value in myself and not in other people. This created a shift in my life but not necessarily for the better. I shifted from Joseph into academia. On the night of my last sessions with her, I ended my relationship with Joseph. We had a real heart to heart. I told him that once I left for graduate school, which was in a couple of weeks, we should call it quits. He walked out visibly upset but I could never have anticipated what happened next.

He was gone for several hours. I assumed he was out with his friends and would be back in the morning. I was concerned for him, so I waited up and eventually fell asleep on the sofa. At about two in the morning, Joseph woke me up. He stood over me looking completely broken. His eyes looked lifeless. He was extremely drunk. I feared he might pass out from alcohol poisoning. I had known him for roughly ten years and I just knew within me that this was his cry for help. We talked and cried together till the sun came up. Eventually we both fell asleep.

I still left him.

The saddest part of this whole episode was that, the person around whom I had built my life and sought validation from, was human after all. He also, like all of us needed help! We have no business depending on human beings for validation. It is upon God alone that we can depend and seek validation.

Ending the relationship was empowering. Moving away was empowering. Cutting everyone off to focus on graduate school was empowering; until I was lonely and like an addict I slipped back into my old ways of seeking validation in other people.

CHAPTER FOUR

JESUÚ

That at the name of Jesus every knee should bow, in heaven and on earth and under the earth, and every tongue acknowledge that Jesus Christ is Lord, to the glory of God the Father.
Philippians 2:10-11 (NIV)

AN ATTEMPT AT A NEW BEGINNING

Graduate school was a very lonely time for me. I had just broken up with Joseph and I had moved into an entirely new environment where I knew virtually no one. I lived a very monastic life in my first year. My home was a studio apartment and I slept in a sleeping bag. My life was regimented between school, work, the gym and believe it or not, church.

The town I moved to, is probably one of the few places in the USA that has an actual Anglican Church. And so, out of my desire to do something that would make my mother proud, I started attending church there.

I enjoyed it.

I liked the hymns and canticles and the order of worship. It was just like being in Ghana and it made me less homesick and lonely. But it didn't fill that void left by Joseph. I drowned myself in the academics of Mechanical Engineering, spent at least an hour in the gym every day and worked two jobs. I worked as a graduate assistant by day and a pizza maker by night. However, my insecurities persisted. I still needed other people to validate me.

About a year into graduate school, I started feeling inadequate about what kind of engineer I would be, since I had no hands-on experience. Most of the other students either had a bachelor's degree in engineering, or grew up on a farm and had years of hands-on experience. I had neither. One day, I packed bag and baggage, put graduate school on ice and went to Ghana to look for a job as a mechanic.

It seems completely illogical now but back then, it made perfect sense to me.

I worked as a mechanic for a year, initially changing tires and oil but then eventually overhauling entire engines. I was one of two women who worked at Vodi Technik as mechanics. The other lady worked in the body shop. The men were very gracious, they never treated us like 'women'. They teased us along with the guys and helped us when we needed help. Probably, the only time I felt like a girl was when there was something heavy to lift. In those instances, there was always one of the men ready to come to the rescue.

Once, I was sitting in a car that was lifted up for another mechanic to work underneath it. My job was to turn the steering wheel so he could do some checks on the tires. As the car went up and I was looking over the tops of all the other cars, I suddenly realized I had seen the exact scene before. Déjà vu. It was a dream I had had over a decade ago. I remembered the dream because when I woke up, I remember thinking, 'maybe I had died in a car crash and as my spirit was being lifted out of my body, I could see all these cars from the top.' I dismissed it at the time but sitting in that car watching my dream play out in front of me reminded me of when I was eight, and I used to see visions of things that actually happened. When the examination was done, the car came down and I didn't give the incident a second thought.

After a year, I went back to the USA, finished my degree and started attending job fairs in an attempt to find a real job. The USA was in an economic recession at that time, so most companies said they were not hiring but were only present at these fairs in order to maintain good relations with the schools. I felt very lost and vulnerable during those times.

To make matters worse, my father had suffered a stroke and was extremely unwell. I had always been close to him and would often call and share my woes but didn't think I should burden him with my problems at that time. So I just sucked them up. My brother thought I was such a loser that to call him and say I couldn't find a job would just be opening the door for insult to be added to injury.

So I turned to my old faithful friend, God.

We had been on relatively good terms. And since I was going to church and had even fasted for Lent, I figured He would look on me favorably. In those days, I believed in bartering and trading with God. My image of Him had modified significantly from when I was a young child. I now saw him as this large white haired guy waiting to point an accusatory finger at me. I no longer thought of God as being loving, or forgiving, or wanting to hug me. He just wasn't that kind of guy to me anymore. As far as I was concerned, He had metamorphosed into a cold and hard negotiator.

So I negotiated.

One day, I was sitting in my studio apartment, when I got a call from one of my engineering colleagues, Raul, asking whether I'd be attending the 'Cummins Seminar'. He asked the question as if it was common knowledge. But I had never even heard the name Cummins before. Apparently, Cummins was an engine manufacturing company, that came to campus every summer and held a special session for engineering students. Because I'd been away the summer before, I wasn't aware of it. So I asked him to forward me the email he had received on the seminar. I quickly registered and sent my Curriculum Vitae (CV) to the Cummins review board.

That same afternoon, I got an invitation to attend an interview the next day. So I dressed up in the only suit I had and headed out. Each of us was called into a 5-minute interview with a member of the review board. I had very little interview experience so I was petrified. But Raul had assured me that it was just an initial assessment and didn't require excessive preparation. Nonetheless, I reworked and reprinted my CV. This new one was markedly different from the original one I submitted. In wanting to ensure that my greatest achievements, which for me were my education and my job with Proctor & Gamble stood out, I deleted my job as a mechanic with Vodi Tecnik in Ghana.

I walked into the interview room, said hello politely, gave a firm handshake with good eye contact like I'd been taught and sat. My interviewer was a tall, lean man who had a lovely warmth about him. I liked him immediately, so I relaxed and handed him my CV. He looked at it and frowned.

Sounding alarmed he said, "I thought you worked as a mechanic somewhere?"

I was startled and started to explain how it was just a one-year internship in a mechanic shop and how it was nothing like my experience at P&G. His response has stuck with me to this day.

He said, "Do you have any idea how impressed we all were to meet a woman who worked as a mechanic in Africa? We were all jostling to be the one to interview you!"

With that, he pulled up the old CV, the one I had submitted originally. And what was supposed to be a 5-minute interview to assess me, wound up being a 30-minute discussion about what Cummins did and where he thought I could fit in.

Incredible!

> **For my thoughts are not your thoughts, neither are your ways my ways," declares the Lord. Isaiah 55:8 (NIV)**

I left that room dazed. I wasn't even sure of the meaning of what had just transpired. Did I have a job?

Yup! Turns out I did!

Four weeks later, I packed my bags and moved to the Midwest to start my life as a Design Engineer for Cummins Inc.

God had done well, and I let Him know. I went to church to say thank you.

IF GOD IS NOT THE REASON, THEN YOU HAVE NO REASON

Cummins was exciting. The buildings were impressive. The manufacturing plants were huge and automated. It was incredible to see truck engines being manufactured by robotic arms with minimal assistance from humans. Everything was so structured and organized and big!

Of course, it fed my complex, because all of a sudden, I had the confidence to talk to my brother and my friends about the fact that I was now working for a Fortune 500 company and earning a salary that was higher than most people my age. Now my brother could be proud of me.

At Cummins I thrived. And since I had just been blessed with a job, I decided to be a good Christian. I couldn't find an Anglican church but I found an Episcopalian church and started attending that. Given that I was one of a handful, literally, of black people, I was embraced by the church and quickly became involved in leading Bible study. I've always had a knack for explaining things to people, so Bible study for me was not about God or Scripture or any of those things. It was about explaining what I had read.

I also discovered while at Cummins that I had a keen interest in community service, so I started volunteering wherever I could. I volunteered at the shelter for battered women, I served as a Commissioner on the Human Rights Commission of the city, I served on the Advocates for Children Commission, and I served on the African and Africa-American Affinity Group, of which I was eventually made President. I enjoyed all of these activities and they would benefit me greatly later in life but my motives were always selfish. It was to fill the void I felt in me.

Whenever I stopped, I felt lonely and empty, so I kept going. I did everything I could to keep me relevant and appreciated by other people. As I have said before, I was no better than an addict who drowns his sorrows in a bottle or in drugs. My drug of addiction was approval. And I was willing to do any kind of work for a paycheque of approval; professional work, volunteer work, and eventually academic work. That is how I wound up getting a Master's degree in Business Administration (MBA), to receive approval from my colleague, Jerry. He suggested we do it so that he wouldn't have to study alone. It's incredible to think that I spent two years in night school, just so that my friend would think I was a nice person!!

I was so consumed with doing things I thought would increase my status in the eyes of people, when what I should have concentrated on was doing the things that would please God. I should have placed God at the center of all my life and not other people. Without realizing it, I was practicing full-blown idolatry by placing every one as a god before God.

> **You shall have no other gods before me. Exodus 20:3 (NIV)**

GOD SENT A FRIEND

One day, I saw an advert to volunteer for a book fair for underprivileged kids. I signed up immediately and was assigned a slot to man a book table and encourage the kids to read. When I got to my table, there was an Indian lady, about my age or a bit younger sitting there. I asked if I was at the right table, she looked at a list and confirmed it and I sat on the chair next to her.

We exchanged polite pleasantries, chitchatted briefly and just sat quietly for a while. I can't for the life of me, remember what got us talking properly but soon, we were talking about how we grew up. And what we discovered was that, apart from the fact that she is Indian and I am Ghanaian, we had lived almost mirror lives.

We grew up exactly the same way, in Middle Class homes, where both our parents were highly educated professionals and very strict. The one big difference between us was that she was a deeply spiritual Catholic and I...well, at best, was a church going Anglican. Her name is Ambily.

Ambily had a relationship with Jesus that I deeply admired. She called Him 'Jesuú.' She said it in a higher pitch than her normal tone and ended the last 'u' on a higher note than all the other letters. She mentioned His name with such affection, like she was talking about a truly beloved friend. According to her, she heard from Him and would tell me what He said about various situations. Jesus to her was a close friend with a great sense of humor and a very sweet and gentle personality. I certainly had never met that Jesus but I was drawn to Him, so I stayed close to my new friend.

> **I no longer call you servants, because a servant does not know his master's business. Instead, I have called you friends, for everything that I learned from my Father I have made known to you. John 15:15 (NIV)**

Over time, Ambily and I became inseparable and I was so taken by this relationship she had with Jesus that, we did everything together. Fortunately, we both worked for Cummins so it was not difficult for us to spend time together during work hours. Whenever we weren't working in our separate departments, she in Procurement and I in Engineering, we were together. She lived about twenty minutes away from me and so we visited each other often. We would talk late into the night about Jesus and what He had to say about everything. Many nights I slept over at her place.

Up until I met Ambily, I had never considered being friends with Jesus. Which is why this is the first time I am mentioning Him in this book in relationship to me. For me, God had always been my guy. Fatherly and serious with a dry sense of humor but not really a hangout buddy like Jesus was to Ambily. I remember she would make the sign of the cross every time we drove past a church. When I asked her why she always did that, she said it was just an acknowledgment of her friend Jesuú. She didn't care where she was or who she was with, she would stop mid-sentence to cross herself. That is how unashamed she was of Him.

It was beautiful! And I wanted that.

> **God is love. Whoever lives in love lives in God and God in them. 1 John 4:16 (NIV)**

I wanted to be cool with Jesus like that. So one day I told her. I asked her how I could be buddies with Jesus. What she said to me shook me to my core. She said, "first of all you have to stop saying you don't like people."

What!?

That had become my mantra.

I felt so taken advantage of, and hard-done by so many people that, between the hurt I felt and my naturally introverted disposition, I had concluded that my safest place was in solitude. I had learned to quickly cut off anyone who did or said anything that hurt me. Seeing how we are all only just human, that was a lot of people.

In typical me style, I immediately started to debate with her. I couldn't understand what being close friends with Jesus had to do with relationships with other people. After all, what better way to focus on Christ than to be devoid of the stress of human relationships? In her mature Christian way, all she said was that, Jesus is about love and that in loving Him, we must give off love to others. And she left it there.

That has stayed with me till today.

I didn't see it back then but God was slowly breaking down my defenses. It amazes me how well God knows each of us and knows exactly when and through whom to expose us to the truths of life.

I pondered over this 'loving other people' issue for weeks and then one day, in one of our late night conversations, I told Ambily that I was willing to open up to people but I needed her to show me what to do to be close to Jesus.

She smiled very softly and said, "Let's just pray and ask Him."

Somehow, that was not what I expected. I thought she would call Him and just tell Him. After all she was constantly having these open conversations with Jesuú. I just thought she would simply tell Him.

I knew how to pray in general but when she said let us pray, I felt deeply uncomfortable. So I asked her to pray as an example. Her prayer that evening changed my approach to prayer completely. She just chatted with Jesus. She acknowledged Him as God but her prayer had neither the formality of a typical orthodox prayer nor the floweriness of a charismatic prayer. It was simply a request from one dear friend to another.

So then I also prayed. Quietly. My prayer was also casual but much more timid. I was talking to a man I didn't know too well and I quite frankly felt a little bashful and foolish about the whole thing. I simply said, "Jesus I want You to be my friend, like how You are friends with Ambily. I want to be able to tell You everything and feel You around me all the time. Amen."

As I knelt there by Ambily's sofa praying, I felt this overwhelming presence. I can't describe it except to say that it filled me with such peace and joy that it made me cry. And it made me feel cold. Not freezing cold but cold like you would feel from the breeze of an Autumn evening, or the breeze of a Harmattan morning. Cold like I felt when I was eight. It made me cry. It still makes me cry.

You will fill me with joy in your presence, with eternal pleasures at your right hand. Psalm 16:11 (NIV)

I wish I had recorded that date, because if there is a day I can mark as being born-again, that was probably it. I only remember that it was a Friday. I do not remember how long I knelt there but Ambily left and went to her room. After a while, I got up and went and lay on Ambily's bed and told her what I felt. She had this small winning smile on the corner of her lips but said nothing.

That evening, just about five hundred meters from the gate of my home, a policeman pulled me over and gave me a ticket for improperly passing an emergency vehicle. That's the kind of offence you normally get a warning for but he was so harsh and unkind to me, especially in the way he spoke to me. It was as if we had some issue before this encounter. I graciously accepted my fine but my spirit was deeply dampened, so I called Ambily who immediately started laughing.

And she said, "You don't expect to give your life to Christ and walk away scot-free do you?" That was my first lesson in "Introduction to Spiritual Attacks 101." When I got home, I lay in my sofa, no lights, no TV and I spent the rest of the evening talking to Jesus. I had a lot to say. He didn't say much except to give me a warm embrace. All throughout the weekend I could feel Him all around me.

For the first time in years, my void was filled and the loneliness was gone. Up until that time, I listened to every genre of music except gospel music. I was however very familiar with gospel music because I had sung in a gospel choir in university. So I went online and downloaded some of the songs I remembered and filled my home with them. To date, those two days in that brand new relationship with Jesus are still amongst the best days of my life. The peace, the tranquility and the love were so overwhelming.

In Jesus I had discovered a friend. A friend who had been knocking at the gate of my heart for years. But the vicissitudes of life had prevented me from hearing Him, let alone open up my heart to Him. Ambily was a good friend but Jesus was an absolutely amazing friend to have found.

In the poem 'What a friend we have in Jesus' written by Joseph M. Scriven to his mother, there is a line that reads "In his arms he'll take and shield thee, Thou wilt find a solace there."

That poem, later a popular hymn, is one I had known all my life but that weekend was the first time it made any practical sense to me.

Jesus is indeed our friend, a true confidant. One we can trust and count on at all times and in all situations. He is on constant standby to join our club of friends. And it is a marvelous experience to have Him be part of the team. I pray that everyone at some point in their life experiences this.

What a friend we have in Jesus
All our sins and griefs to bear
And what a privilege to carry
Everything to God in prayer!

IN THE MIDST OF PLENTY, THE FOOL IS HUNGRY

I started attending church with more purpose from then on, or so I thought. One day, I went to a Catholic church with Ambily. After Mass, she asked me what I thought of the sermon. The question surprised me because I didn't realize I was supposed to think anything of the sermon. I had not listened to the sermon or any other sermon for that matter. So after over twenty years of attending church and hearing sermons, I started listening to them.

Unfortunately, I found many of them of absolutely no relevance to me. I struggled to understand how they related to me, or even what I was supposed to do with them when I left church. Being such a practical hands-on person, I was looking for the priest to give me implementable solutions. But mostly I heard about how I needed to repent, because I was a sinful person. It wasn't encouraging. So as hard as I tried, I soon found myself drifting away from church. But I held onto Jesus.

My life for the next few years was very grounded. I was doing very well at work. I finished my MBA, moved into a job in procurement, bought a house and I was happy. But I wasn't married and this became the new source of disappointment for my mother.

My singleness somehow got an honorable mention in every phone call no matter the topic. This became a great source of pain and distress for me. On hindsight, I clearly was still not completely confident in myself. Although I had developed this relationship with Christ, there was still so much about the Christian faith I did not understand. I didn't know how to rely on God in my difficulties. I only knew to pray, because that was all that Ambily had taught me. I read my Bible but I read it as I did my children's Bible. I didn't realize that the Biblical stories are intended to speak to real life situations and give us examples of how God intervenes in our lives and the lessons we are to learn.

More importantly, I did not realize that my newly found relationship with Jesus meant that I had everything, literally. If He is the Son of God and the center of our universe, then being His friend meant I could have access to anything I needed. Not anything I wanted but anything I needed. So although everybody wanted me to get married, the fact that I was not married at that point meant my friend Jesus did not think I needed marriage at that time. I should have taken solace in the fact that God knew what was best for me and His plans for me were not man's plans for me.

If I knew those things, I would never have fretted about not being married. I would never have cared that my mother and several 'concerned' relatives essentially implied by their commentary that I was inadequate and incomplete as a woman if I was not married and did not have children.

I took such pride in being a highly educated, hard-working and upward moving woman, all of which was constantly negated by the lack of a husband. Yet in Scripture, many of the women who were closest to God were single. Women like Miriam and Lydia just to mention a couple.

There are several young women out there today who are hurting because they are not praised and encouraged for being productive citizens. Rather, they are condemned for not being married. And yet each of us as women, especially Christian women, aspire to be like the Proverbs thirty-one woman. The thing about the Proverbs thirty-one woman is that in the twenty-one verses of Proverbs 31:10-31, what the Scripture talks about is how wonderfully amazing this woman is as an *individual*.

Nowhere does the Scripture ascribe her virtues to the fact that she was married. She was handling her business long before she was married. She made her husband proud, she added value to him, she made him look good. And all that was because she was a complete person doing her own thing before she became a partner to him. In other words, she became a full and complete woman (human) before she was attached to any man. The idea of marriage is not to make us whole. It is to give us a partner. A partner who is also whole. So that the two wholes through the mysterious sacrament of marriage become one under one God, to serve His purpose. Any other agenda for marriage is not God's plan and does not qualify to be categorized under "what God has put together."

I, of course, had not even read Proverbs thirty-one at the time. So I just fretted about what the world thought and I felt angry with God for not giving me what I 'needed'. I got so miserable with this situation that, I decided to move back to Ghana where I was more likely to meet eligible Ghanaian men. At the time, I was very adamant about marrying a Ghanaian. I'm not quite sure what the rationale was but that was my thing then. The only barrier between myself and Ghana was my house. I tried everything legal under the sun to get rid of that house but it just didn't work. The house just would not 'move.' It was as if God had closed the door to the house selling. Eventually, I gave up and I set out to get married regardless.

It was a very academic exercise for me, where I made a list of the qualities I was looking for in a man. Strangely, despite my own budding relationship with Christ, I never included in my list that the man needed to have a relationship with Christ. The list was based solely on what my mother said was important, a good job and a nice man. Whatever that meant. So I created an excel sheet of all the men pursuing me at the time and one of them stood out. And we got married!!

FORCING ISSUES WITH GOD

All Anglican weddings begin with the words,

> *"Dearly beloved, we are gathered together here in the sight of God and in the face of His congregation, to join together this man and this woman in holy matrimony, which is an honorable estate, instituted of God in paradise in the time of man's innocence, signifying unto us the mystical union, that is between Christ and his Church: which holy estate Christ adorned and beautified with His presence and first miracle that He performed in Cana of Galilee and is commended of Saint Paul to be honorable among all men and therefore is not to be entered into unadvisedly, lightly, or wantonly, to satisfy men's carnal lusts and appetites, like brute beasts that have no understanding but reverently, discreetly, advisedly, soberly and in the fear of God, duly considering the causes for which matrimony was ordained."*

As a priest, whenever I'm officiating a wedding, I slow down and say very deliberately the words, *"not to be entered into unadvisedly, lightly, or wantonly, but reverently, discreetly, advisedly, soberly and in the fear of God."* But I can tell from the excited looks on the faces of all the couples into whose eyes I stare and say these words that it is completely lost on them and they can't hear a word I'm saying. But I don't blame them, because in all honesty, I don't ever recall hearing those words although I myself got married in an Anglican church. Sometimes I think the reason I say these particular words so intently is partly as an apology to God for the depth of the foolishness with which I entered into marriage and probably also as a life-line to the couple in front of me just in case they are being as foolish as I was.

But there I was, now dating a man I quite liked but with whom I was not in love. And with whom I was not really friends. I reminded myself of all the stress I had felt with Joseph and convinced myself that marriage was not about being in love. It was about being sensible, and as far as I was concerned, Seth represented all that was sensible and not frivolous in a man. That was what I believed would make my mother happy, so I set about making sure that he fitted into some criteria that my mother would approve of. And I never took the time to actually get to know him. I essentially spent most of our dating life trying to groom him for my mum, and not celebrating him for who he was. I can only imagine how miserable it all was for him and how disrespected he must have felt. But all the same he endured and we decided to get married.

I spoke to Jesus several times about Seth but He was strangely quiet. I would spend hours in the shower asking over and over if He was happy with my decision and my choice but there was no warm hug. And no cool breeze. There was just silence. He wasn't distant, just quiet. So one day I concluded that silence meant consent and I stopped asking Him.

Given that we'd met in the USA, there was no way we could just show up in Ghana and get married. It was important that we met each other's folks. We agreed to fly to Ghana for a few days, meet the folks and then come back and start planning the wedding.

We headed out to the airport to catch a flight to Accra via New York and that's when the weirdness began. The first strange incident was that at the airport where we were simply catching a domestic flight to New York, we were stopped because my yellow fever card had expired. To begin with, it was very strange that yellow fever came up at a domestic US airport. That notwithstanding, this could easily have been dealt with in Ghana by me being given a shot at the Ghana airport. It was actually quite standard but this woman at the counter simply wasn't having it. She refused to let us pass and in the end the Ministry of Interior in Ghana had to be called to resolve the matter. Two hours later, the matter was resolved but we had missed our flight and ended up going back home to Seth's apartment.

That night Seth told me that the devil was trying to prevent us from getting married. With a faith that was no more than a candle in the wind, I agreed with him and we spent the night binding and casting all kinds of marriage-preventing-demons. Poor demons, they must have been terribly puzzled by it all! Not once did it strike me that God was answering my prayer and cautioning me, quite loudly I might add, that this was not His preferred path for my life.

The next day, we took off and managed to get to Ghana. My mother and my brother didn't like Seth. At all. But I thought their reasons were frivolous and highfalutin, so despite my own doubts about how I felt, I held on more strongly to him. Again, God was talking, this time through my mother. But I wasn't listening. I met his family and his father didn't like me. But Seth felt his reasons were prejudicial and unfair and he also ignored his father. Again, God spoke and I missed it. We returned to the USA feeling triumphant, as though we had won a battle and went into full wedding planning mode.

HERE COMES THE BRIDE...AMIDST GOD'S FINAL CAUTION

I have never been a fan of weddings and had never looked forward to one of my own. I had always imagined I'd elope and not have to deal with the funfair of it all. But clearly that is not what was about to happen so I needed to plan a wedding. I essentially let my mother plan it, so in the end, apart from four people whom I invited, everyone else on my side was a friend or a relative of my parents. And there were over one hundred people present.

Interestingly, Ambily and I got married on the same day, so we didn't get a chance to attend each other's wedding, let alone be each other's bridesmaid like we had planned. I felt happy on my wedding day. I was hopeful that I would eventually fall hopelessly in love with Seth. To crown it all, I was especially relieved that my mother could now be listed amongst her friends as one of the ones whose daughter got married. The next step was to make her a grandmother, then I was sure I would win her full approval. But before that God had one last comment about me getting married.

We headed back to the USA a few days later and that was when I finally heard God speak about the marriage.

We flew back with another couple, Barry and Tamara. Both of them had been a year behind me at GIS and it was nice to have familiar faces in a strange land. They were flying back from holiday in Ghana with their young son. And between the five of us we had quite a bit of luggage. They lived about fifteen minutes away from the airport, where Seth had parked our car. We agreed that when we landed, Seth and Barry would leave the airport in our car, drive over to their place, to pick up their car and come back to get the ladies, the baby and our luggage. It seemed like a simple enough plan, until one hour later, the guys hadn't returned.

Tamara and I started to worry, because the whole exercise should not have taken more than thirty minutes. Even with the snow which had started to fall just after we landed, it shouldn't have exceeded an hour. To make things worse, neither Seth nor Barry was answering their phone. Tamara had the baby strapped to her, so I offered to take a cab to their place to see if I could find them. Just as I stepped out of the airport building to find a taxi, Barry pulled up alone in his car. I looked behind him to see if I'd see Seth roll up but he wasn't there. Barry rushed out of the car and grabbed me by the shoulders and said, "First of all Seth is fine. He's not hurt."

"What?! What's going on?" I asked anxiously.

"He was in a head on collision. The car is totalled but he is fine." Barry continued by saying that he had to wait for the cops and that somehow he had left his phone on the kitchen counter when he picked up his keys and Seth had lost his phone in the wreck. I was completely dumbfounded. How could this have happened?

We loaded our luggage into his car and drove to the site of the crash. He dropped me off just outside the area cordoned off by the police and said he was going to drop off Tamara and the baby and would be back. As I walked towards the accident, the first piece of debris I saw was one of the shock absorber springs from Seth's car. As an engineer and a former mechanic, I knew that for the shock absorber spring to come off a vehicle meant the car must have been in a truly devastating accident. As I looked at that spring, the thought of the yellow fever card fiasco flashed through my mind and it suddenly hit me that maybe God had never wanted this marriage for me.

I saw Seth talking to the police and I dismissed the thought and quickened my gait. When he saw me, he paused and looked at me in a way I will never forget. It was a fleeting look of deep disdain, a blend of hate and regret. As though he felt being married to me was a mistake and was the source of all his pain. I would see that look many times before we were finally divorced. But just as quickly as I dismissed my thoughts, he dismissed his and ran to embrace me.

He was clearly shaken, as though he had seen his life flash before his eyes. He gushed about what had happened and how he thought he would die. I tried as best as I could to calm him down and we prayed right there in the freezing cold. The police offered us a warm car to sit in while they hauled off the other driver. She was drunk. As we waited at the back of the cop car, we prayed and promised to love each other no matter what.

That night I couldn't sleep. The image of the shock absorber spring kept playing in my mind. The more I thought through our relationship and how I didn't feel 'in love,' and how my mum and my brother didn't approve of him and his dad didn't approve of me, the surer I was that I had made a mistake.

As I lay there next to my new husband, I felt scared and very alone and very empty. And I wondered, if I had forced God's hand.

But when they said, "Give us a king to lead us," this displeased Samuel; so he prayed to the Lord. And the Lord told him: "Listen to all that the people are saying to you; it is not you they have rejected but they have rejected me as their king. As they have done from the day I brought them up out of Egypt until this day, forsaking me and serving other gods, so they are doing to you. Now listen to them; but warn them solemnly and let them know what the king who will reign over them will claim as his rights." 1 Samuel 8:6-9 (NIV)

CHAPTER FIVE

THE DAYS OF SILENCE

**This is a profound mystery—but I am talking about
Christ and the church. However, each one of you also
must love his wife as he loves himself and the wife
must respect her husband.
Ephesians 5:32-33 (NIV)**

MARRIAGE; AN INSTITUTION LIKE NO OTHER

Seth and I struggled to adjust to each other. We fought constantly. The worst part for me was that each fight would result in several days where he would not speak to me. That was very difficult for me to understand because, I'm such a compartmentalized person that I can park an issue and proceed with life as usual and address the issue later. But it was not so for him and each time he went quiet on me felt like the rejection I was so familiar with from my GIS days. I would therefore resort to begging and pleading with him for forgiveness in order that he would speak to me again and ultimately approve of me. It got to a point where, what we argued about was irrelevant. What was important was that his silent treatment was my fault and I needed to appease him. I began to dread the "days of silence", as I called them, and soon I found myself living in constant fear of offending him.

I was so ill equipped for marriage. And given that my mother and brother did not approve of him, I had absolutely no one to turn to for advice or guidance. As Christians, we often underestimate the importance of marriage discipleship while we are still single. All my training as a young person had been geared towards academic and professional success. And given how well I was doing, I was obviously very well trained. But it was only after I failed at my marriage that I started to attend marriage seminar and now see how truly valuable they are for young people. I believe that any person who embarks on the journey of marriage fueled only by 'love' or 'pressure' is embarking on a dangerous journey filled with misery.

It is critical that as parents, mentors, priests and guardians we take off the kiddy gloves and do away with the political correctness. We need to take the time off to instruct our children and those we shepherd in what to look for in a partner, how to resolve conflict, how to praise and correct a spouse, how to endure through the struggles of marriage and most importantly how to recognize, adjust to, and compliment the individuality of their spouse. I know we often laugh about men being from Mars and women being from Venus. But be that as it may, it is critical for every person who is considering marriage, or who is in a struggling marriage to recognize that men and women are completely different from each other. And yet we can coexist beautifully together as long as we each recognize, appreciate, leverage, applaud and indeed enjoy those differences.

But at the time, I found all those differences confusing and very stressful. Unfortunately, that was when both Seth and I made the most fundamental and most devastating mistake many couples make in marriage. We started talking to our friends about our problems and seeking advice from them. That just poured jet fuel on the already volatile situation. By a year into our marriage, I was three months pregnant and we were barely on speaking terms.

We were both miserable. Everything was a source of conflict. The only happy topic was the constant banter about whether we were having a son or a daughter. I wanted a son and he wanted a daughter and we agreed not to find out.

In my ninth month, my mother showed up to help me with the baby. I was riddled with nervousness because I didn't want her to see how unhappy we were. But the depth of our misery was such that you could sense it just by walking through our front door. Somehow, she didn't discuss it with me. I suppose she expected me to bring it up. I didn't. I just waited for the baby.

IT'S A GIRL!

Seth was wonderful during my labor. He stayed by my side all nine hours and cut the umbilical cord when our daughter Oduma was born. Having a baby is one of the most amazing experiences of my life. It fascinated me how I instantly fell in love with and was willing to give up everything including my very life for this little person whom I didn't know. I suppose that this was the kind of love, that led God to take the life of His own Son in order that we will be saved. I found the birthing process itself extraordinarily painful. Especially since I opted for a natural birth with absolutely no medication. I have heard it said that women forget their pain after they give birth. I still remember mine!!

I gave birth on my mother's birthday and Seth had the forethought to buy her a birthday card on behalf of himself, our daughter and me. But that wasn't the amazing part, he bought an inkpad and used the footprint of our one-hour old baby to stamp the card before he gave it to my mother. That was the sweetness about him that I enjoyed but it was so fleeting that when I think back on our marriage now, all I remember is constantly feeling afraid of an outburst from him.

As I pushed my baby out, I thought to myself from the perspective of an engineer, that as the Ultimate Engineer, God should have come up with a better process for childbirth! But I have come to relate the process of child birth to the mystery of born-again Christian salvation. I had always assumed that after nine months, a child is born whether the child likes it or not. But apparently, that is not so. Like a sinner, a child in the womb must decide first to be born, before it can be born. In the same vein, to be born-again requires a decision to repent and turn away, or leave a particular lifestyle and come into the light of Christ.

That decision by the child triggers a hormone which then begins the labor process. When a child does not make this decision, labor has to be induced. That is when the struggle begins between the world of the womb and the fluorescent lit world of the hospital ward, or the lantern lit room of the village floor. In the same way, when we decide to give our lives to Christ, a battle begins between the world and the light of Christ.

On the maternity bed, it takes the discipleship of trained nurses and doctors to guide that baby from the darkness of the womb to the light of the world. For the same reason, a properly discipled or trained person must guide each of us out of the darkness and into the light in order for us to become born-again Christians. Otherwise, we may enter the light but we would have died in the darkness. Note that I didn't say a priest, or prophet, or man of God must lead us from the darkness into a light. I deliberately said a properly discipled person. Because unless we are in the hands of one who has been properly trained as Jesus trained Peter and John, and as Paul trained Timothy, we will find ourselves manhandled by people who are half baked in Scripture and have not truly received power from the Holy Spirit.

Just as we verify and ask for references about a doctor or a hospital before we submit our bodies to them, so should we ask about men and women of God before we submit our souls to them.

> **But you must remain faithful to the things you have been taught. You know they are true, for you know you can trust those who taught you. 2 Timothy 3:14 (NIV)**

That day, when Oduma was handed over to me, I was struck at how dark she was. She was so dark it was difficult to distinguish between her skin and her hair. Admittedly, I'd only seen a few newborn babies at that point in my life but all of them were very fair, or pale and blotchy.

The next morning, a doctor I'd never seen before woke me up and said that there had been a 'small' problem with the birth, which she needed to explain to me. She turned out to be a pediatrician. She explained to me that Oduma's clavicle was broken. I wasn't quite sure what a clavicle was but the fact that anything was broken in my new baby was enough to make me cry. It turns out a clavicle is the collarbone. Shortly after that meeting, a series of specialist came through, examined Oduma and then went off and talked in hushed tones.

That morning, for the first time in a long while, I had a sincere talk with God. We had been talking a little bit but after His inability or rather refusal to comment on my marriage, I had resorted to telling Him stuff but not listening much. But now I felt I was in trouble and I needed Him to step in. And I was willing to listen.

We spent the next few days taking a series of X-Rays. And when I saw the image of my daughter's clavicle, broken into two parts and separated, I was devastated. To make things worse, the doctors expressed a concern that if the fracture affected the nerve, the arm could be rendered useless. There was no treatment the doctor could offer. He simply said, "Over time, bone will grow around the injury and it will heal." He assured me that in two years' time I would never know that it ever broke as long as the nerve was unaffected.

My mother and Seth were a comfort to have around but all I yearned for was for Ambily's Jesuú to hold onto me and comfort me. He did. And He kept telling me everything would be fine. But I just couldn't imagine how those tiny bones, a centimeter apart, were ever going to come together again.

I can only describe as miraculous what happened over the next few weeks, as far as this injury was concerned. As if by magic, a massive lump of bone grew around the injury. I'm sure for doctors this is very normal but for me, it was a total miracle. Her body just knew to grow new bone where this gap was! As the months went by, the lump of bone started to diminish and take the shape of a collarbone. It added a new dimension of awesomeness to my view of God. But it did not take away any of the anger I felt towards Him for not saying anything about my marriage when I had asked Him. I look back now on my level of arrogance and pride and it fascinates me that God just didn't send down one quick bolt of lightning to strike me down and shut me up forever!

But that is the beauty of God. When Christ was nailed to the cross He pleaded with God the Father to forgive us, because we did not know what we were doing. In that plea, He wasn't necessarily talking just about the Romans nailing Him to the cross.

He was talking about every single one of us who in ignorance says and does things that deeply offend God.

> **In the past God overlooked such ignorance, but now he commands all people everywhere to repent. Acts 17:30 (NIV)**

Now that I had a daughter, I had become a "complete" woman in the eyes of my family and society. I was educated, well employed, married and now a mother.

And yet something felt off.

There was a constant unspoken tension between my mother and my husband. And because of my own insecurities, I tried to please them both. Over time, I began to dislike them both. I tried to play both sides. I defended my husband to my mother in an effort to impress her and show her that I had made the right choice. And then I'd turn around and agree with my husband's condemnation of my mother and my entire family in an effort to please him.

I felt so empty and sad all the time. So I focused on loving my daughter. It was strange, because on the outside, everything was perfect. We were a young married couple and therefore supposed to be happy. We lived in a beautiful lakefront property and were presumed rich. And we had been blessed with a beautiful baby girl and therefore had been 'fruitful.' But within me, all I felt was disdain for my life and towards my God whom I blamed for making my life so miserable.

> **You say, 'I am rich. I have everything I want. I don't need a thing!' And you don't realize that you are wretched and miserable and poor and blind and naked. So I advise you to buy gold from Me—gold that has been purified by fire. Then you will be rich.**

> **Also buy white garments from Me so you will not be shamed by your nakedness and ointment for your eyes so you will be able to see. Revelation 3:17-18 (NLT)**

THINGS FALL APART

A few months after Oduma's birth, I moved to Ghana as planned. Seth and I had agreed that I should take a one year leave-of-absence from work to take care of our new baby. Cummins graciously agreed to give me back my job whenever I returned. But as fate would have it I would never live in the USA again.

The first few months were fine. Seth and I spoke every day, mostly about the baby and what the baby needed. The year before, as part of preparation towards our final move to Ghana, we had established a company in Ghana. So Seth had routinely been coming to Ghana every six to eight weeks. So I still got to see him quite often despite my move but most importantly, he got to see his daughter. As the novelty of it all wore off, we returned to our normal routine of arguing, followed by "the days of silence." The silence now had very little impact on me because it just meant he didn't call and wouldn't take my calls. I no longer had to contend with living in a house with a person who wasn't speaking to me.

But soon it changed. And the silence became threats of divorce. They frightened me. I didn't know what to do. I couldn't tell my mother because it would prove her right. I was too embarrassed to tell anyone except Kofi Boateng.

Kofi and I had met ten years earlier when I was in my first year of university. I had come home for Christmas holidays and one of the few GIS people I liked, Grace, who had stayed in Ghana, invited me to spend a few days with her at her university, the Kwame Nkrumah University of Science and Technology

(Tech).

I was excited to have the opportunity to experience campus life in Ghana. The conditions were very different from my university in the USA. In the USA I had one roommate but here several students shared a room. But I loved the fact that everyone was Ghanaian and could relate to me and vice versa. There was a feeling of camaraderie and acceptance that I definitely did not feel at my university and had not even experienced at GIS.

Things at Tech were so simple and down to earth. And I wished I could have stayed there and just become a student. But I only had four days. Kofi, one of Grace's friends, immediately took a fancy to me and made it his job to ensure that I had the best four days ever. He had a nice build and was handsome. And it amused me how often he would tell me that he was handsome! I liked him very much and thoroughly enjoyed his company. When I returned to the USA, we stayed in touch and when he graduated, he came to the USA for graduate school. Overtime, we became very close friends and confidants.

He had moved back to Ghana a year before I did and when I came to Ghana, he was one of the people I leaned heavily on for guidance as a returnee. One day, after one of my fights with Seth, where he yelled down the phone about how frustrated and tired and unhappy he was with being married to me, I called Kofi and wept bitterly. I told him everything and he asked that we meet. We met and talked for hours. Kofi comforted me, prayed with me and did all the things I had hoped Jesus would do. I didn't realize then that Kofi was just the vessel Jesus was using.

It's a shame how little credit we give God for what He does for us. God is never going to come and physically bail us out or comfort us. He is always going to use one of His vessels. But unfortunately, so many of us get so enamored with the vessel that we tend to think the people who have helped us are our salvation and we forget about God. That was me. Kofi was my salvation and as far as I was concerned, Jesus needed to take a cue from him and step up His game.

After we spoke, he asked me if I'd accompany him to a breakfast meeting for Christians. I was hesitant because in as much as I was interested in God, I did not believe in open demonstrations of faith. It felt like they were just demonstration to the whole world, so that everyone would think we are pious.

The name alone was a turn off for me; Full Gospel Business Men's Fellowship International. It sounded like one of the many new-fangled churches where people got together to pray loudly and added the word 'international' to give their group some credibility. But just before I could decline he said, "you know I really didn't want to go when I was invited but I did and I was amazed at the people who were a part of it..."

"Like who?" I challenged.

"Do you know Pakwo Shum?" he asked. Before he could continue, I interrupted him out of sheer disbelief, "Pakwo is a member!?"

"Yeah he was there. In fact he is the chapter president."

I didn't know then what a chapter president was but I knew that Pakwo was my senior at GIS and was a very successful businessman. There was no way he would be a part of a frivolous Christian group, unless something had really changed with him. On the basis of that one name alone, I agreed to attend the breakfast meeting the next Saturday morning at the Holiday Inn.

And it changed my life.

I have heard it said, that sometimes our life and our lifestyle is the only Bible someone else will read. I'm sure Pakwo wasn't living his life with the intention of making a convert out of me but that is what happened. All of us are constantly being watched by people we don't know. And what we do or don't do can make the difference in whether they find salvation or not. I didn't even know Pakwo was a Christian. I just knew that he was a respectable person and so I was willing to follow his lead.

> **Choose a good reputation over great riches; being held in high esteem is better than silver or gold. Proverbs 22:1 (NLT)**

FULL GOSPEL BUSINESS MEN'S FELLOWSHIP INTERNATIONAL

That breakfast meeting changed my perspective as far as what it means to live as a Christian is concerned. That was the first time I saw respectable, credible, people in society openly profess Christ by sharing their stories of sin and foolishness. And telling publicly how they had come to see the light of Christ and change their ways. I saw grown men openly cry in gratitude for what God had delivered them from. It was a truly mind blowing experience.

That day, although Pakwo didn't speak, he was at the head table, clearly endorsing what was going on. After the main speaker spoke, he asked if those present had something they wanted prayed about. A number of people went forward, so I went along expecting a general prayer. But instead, all the men at the head table, stood up, walked up to us and then one by one, took our hands and asked us in secret what was bothering us. I wasn't sure I could trust the whole process, so when it came to my turn, I only whispered in the man's ear that my daughter had broken her collar bone. He nodded, looked at me with the most compassionate eyes and then prayed. He prayed as if he and God were comrades and he was briefing Him on a situation for which he expected God to take immediate action.

This was a whole new type of Christianity, that I was just not familiar with. I had grown up always praying quietly and privately. Prayer was not a thing to be shared. Even Ambily and I when we prayed together didn't share the prayer. But somehow this idea of sharing concerns and praying about them with someone was very reassuring. I suddenly wished I had told him my real problem, which was my marriage.

I left the breakfast meeting exhilarated and full of hope for my marriage. I imagined that I'd tell Seth all about it and encourage him to join. He had been very active in the Scripture Union while he was in university and I just knew he would enjoy the fellowship. Not to mention the opportunity to meet other Finance people like himself. In that moment of hope, I somehow managed to drop the constant fear I had of offending him and I called him. The phone rang and then suddenly cut. Then I remembered that we were still in the days of silence from the last fight. Feeling upset, I went home and comforted myself by watching Oduma sleep. And then I fell asleep.

As time went on I realized that with each fight, I was slipping into a depression. I felt like I was losing myself. All I wanted to do was sleep so that I wouldn't have to fight, or apologize, or wonder what I was doing wrong. The only thing that kept me going was my daughter and this deep need I felt within me to give her as good a life as my parents had given me or better. But with each threat of divorce, my ability to be a good mother and wife fell further into the darkness of depression. One day, I asked Kofi if he thought Seth really wanted a divorce or if he was just using the threat to frighten and control me.

"There's only one way to find out. But you may not like what you discover," he answered cautiously.

"Okaaay. I'm listening," I said equally cautiously.

"It's simple, the next time he asks for a divorce, agree to it. If he accepts it, then he really wants out. But if he backs down, then you will know that he's just been calling your bluff." Then he warned me and said, "But don't do it unless you're willing to deal with the consequences of what he says."

I decided not to try it.

I decided instead to go to the USA and spend some time with Seth. I assumed, or maybe I had hoped that his attitude was because he missed me and was acting out. I couldn't have been more wrong.

The day I arrived, I discovered the real reason for the constant threat to our marriage and it resulted in a terrible fight between us. We yelled at each other and past what we each really needed. In the end it descended into a very bitter war of insults, that went beyond us to our parents, our friends and all the people and things we were associated with. I had not realized how much hatred had developed between us in just two short years. It was as if neither one of us had anything that they even marginally liked about the other.

It was almost midnight when I called my mother. And for the first time told her all that I had been through over the past two years. She was very calm and simply asked that I calm down, find a safe place to stay away from Seth and just come back home to Ghana. Despite my fear that she would condemn me, she never did. She simply said, "you people have a daughter to raise and that is what you have to focus on."

That statement strengthened me and has been one of the guiding principles by which I live. Whenever it comes to making any decision about this child that I have with a man with whom I have had such a hard relationship, that statement gives me clarity.

It reminds me of what is important. She is primary. Above my pain, above my pride. Above myself.

I heeded my mum's advice and stayed with my close friends, Dawn and Gil Palmer. A few days later, I flew back to Ghana. I was so low that I couldn't imagine that there could be a lower point. But there was.

BE CAREFUL WHAT YOU WISH FOR

Seth called and said he wanted to put everything behind us. He said he would be coming to Ghana the next week so we could sit and talk and try to save our marriage. But when after a month he hadn't shown up, the fights picked up again and with them renewed threats of divorce. They wore on me and eventually I was so raw with pain and fear that one day I said to him, "I hate that I make you so miserable, so I'll grant you a divorce."

The silence on the other end of the phone was deafening. Then I heard the beeping of a disengaged phone. He had hung up.

I panicked and called Kofi, who said, "give him time, he will call back with his decision."

I couldn't sit still. I tried to breastfeed the baby because I found it very soothing. But she was sleepy and didn't want to eat. So I decided to go to the gym. On my way, Seth called. "This is not what I want" he said. "I don't want a divorce." I was in disbelief.

It's hard to place a finger on what emotion I felt in that moment. I'm not sure whether it was anger, or grief, or a combination of both. But whatever it was, I felt my heart freeze over. As if someone had poured a slushy frozen liquid down the main artery to my heart and just cooled it to a slow steady pulse.

What I felt for him in that moment went far beyond hatred. It was apathy. I just didn't care. I felt bullied, betrayed and insulted. All I said was, "I'm going to the gym now so I'll call you later." The rest of the day was like an out of body experience, where I could feel myself poking and prodding my heart, begging it to feel something. But I felt nothing.

WHAT MARRIAGE IS SUPPOSED TO BE

The divine reality hidden in the metaphor of marriage is that God ordained a permanent union between His Son and the church. Marriage therefore is about sacrifice. It is the earthly image of God's divine plan for Christ and the church to become one body. Just as the husband and wife are to become one flesh.

I believe this means that as women and wives, we should take our cue in marriage from the church's subjection to Christ. And men should take theirs from Christ's love for the church. So as husbands, men have the responsibility to lead with the kind of love that is willing to die in order that the wife may live. I mean that in the sense of self-sacrifice and a willingness to deny their desires in order that their wives can thrive. But today, the harmony of marriage has been ruined by both men and women. Some men's loving leadership has deteriorated into hostile domination in some cases and lazy indifference in others. Many of us women, as we have become more educated and self-sufficient, have misconstrued willing submission to be a lack of intelligence. And as a result, some of us have become obsequiously manipulative, while others of us have become brazenly defiant.

But one read through the book of Esther makes clear that it is the intelligent woman who submits in order that she may lead her king to a place where he acquiesces to her every whim.

So many of us are so preoccupied with the worldly trappings of marriage; the wedding, the 'legal sex,' the financial benefits of having more than one income; that we forget that marriage is actually a sacrament. It has its physical manifestations like the ring and living together but far more profound is that two souls are joined in the sight of God. I think as parents and as a church, if we processed marriage this way, the last thing we would do is rush our sons and daughters into this spiritual bond or bondage as the case may be, just because society deems a married man responsible and a married woman fulfilled. On the contrary, the height of irresponsibility and un-fulfillment is to enter into marriage unprepared and worse still introduce innocent lives into our mess.

That was me. In a huff to get my mother off my case, I had naïvely entered into this bondage that triggered all the negative habits I had been trying to shed since my secondary school days.

I was so angry and hurt that, I wanted to hurt Seth by walking away and offering him nothing. Not even my hatred. I made my stance clear, that since he had asked for a divorce I was going to ensure that he got one. And with that the battle was on.

The next week, he went to court and filed against me.

THERE'S A REASON WHY GOD HATES DIVORCE

What ensued was a vehement battle that took off with property and landed on who would have custody over our daughter. Everything was a weapon that we used against each other. My house which miraculously sold two weeks after I put it back on the market was the first point of contention. As soon as that was settled the fight became about our company in Ghana. With each issue, I heeded my mother's advice to never fight over property and conceded.

With each concession my net worth plummeted. Then the war shifted to a full blown custody battle over our daughter. That, I was not willing to concede. We fought each other so intensely that our lawyers advised us not to speak to each other anymore.

What was interesting is that, in all of it without ever discussing it, we both instinctively knew that our daughter should not be affected by our difficulties. So I sent him daily pictures to let him know how she was doing and he would often call so she could hear his voice. I had several people tell me during those days and even today that I should keep Oduma away from him to make him suffer. But I never processed it that way. I did not believe then and do not believe now that I or any other parent has the right to prevent a child from knowing or interacting with their other parent.

There's an African adage which says, "when two elephants fight, it is the grass that suffers." In a marriage, that proverbial grass is always the children. In the blindness of our hate, the devil takes advantage and makes us feel as though we're pouring pain onto our spouse, while in reality it is our children we are killing. Every child deserves to know and form a relationship with both parents as long as they are alive and it is safe for the child to do so. Regardless of the choices we may have made as adults, it is God and God alone who chooses the parents of a child and we cannot un-choose it for that child. Even if we disagree.

After a year-long cold war, spotted with moments of open warfare, we got divorced.

There are many schools of thoughts about divorce in terms of what Scripture says and how it is interpreted. As a person who has actually been through a divorce, my preoccupation is not so much with what Scripture says but rather with why Scripture says what it says.

Divorce is painful and I wouldn't wish it on my worst enemy. I have come to believe that it is because of His inordinate love for us that God says He hates divorce. It is because He does not want us to feel such pain that He has put in place so many measures to prevent us from going through such a thing. Divorce robs us of our peace, our self-esteem and as is evident in many mental hospitals, our sanity.

Divorce can damage our children and have repercussions for generations to come. That brokenness between two people who once loved each other, is to the devil what nectar is to a bee. He feeds on it for free and makes honey in the form of bitterness, hatred, confusion, ill-will and damage that his demons feed on for years and years until by the grace of God, Christ steps in to break the cycle.

We therefore as parents and the church must be proactive and not reactive. We must not sit by and watch our children enter into the sacrament of marriage before we either start doing damage control, or insisting that they remain in a situation of undue misery and sometimes danger. We have a responsibility to use Scripture to disciple our children into marriage. And as young people, we have a responsibility to seek to be discipled by more than trendy magazines which tend to focus on the beauty of weddings and say nothing about marriage.

I had no marriage discipleship. Now I was a single mother. And an unemployed one at that.

CHAPTER SIX

A MAN WAS GOING DOWN FROM JERUSALEM TO JERICHO

Jesus said: "A man was going down from Jerusalem to Jericho, when he was attacked by robbers. They stripped him of his clothes, beat him and went away, leaving him half dead."
Luke 10:30 (NIV)

My only anchor was my mother.

WE ARE ALL SUSCEPTIBLE

She was a solid rock for me but I missed my father. He had died three years earlier. Exactly three months after I got married. He was too unwell to walk me down the aisle, and I remember asking him if he was happy that I was getting married. He couldn't talk so he nodded, but given that he never really got to know my husband, I'm not sure what he was nodding to. Whatever it was, ninety days later he was dead. And I no longer had access to his counsel.

My father and I always had a quiet but close relationship. I say quiet because most of the time we spent together was spent in silence listening to classical music. He was very calm and measured in everything he did. I've often wondered how he would have reacted to how my life has played out and especially to my priesthood. I'll never know but suffice it to say, I miss him and I hope he's proud of me.

At the time, I felt devastated and ashamed at the fact that I had failed at my marriage. I was filled with guilt that I had rendered my child a statistic. She would now join the ranks of 'those' children brought up by a single parent. Or as people like to term it 'in a broken home'. I discovered that in as much as people are sympathetic towards a person who has lost a spouse to death, there is not a second thought spared to a person who has lost a spouse to divorce. What we must recognize is that while the cause of the loss is different, it is a loss nonetheless. And a person goes through a grieving process as well and therefore we must have compassion.

What happens in reality is that while the person who has lost a spouse to death draws a lot of love and compassion, the one who has lost a spouse to divorce draws hate and condemnation. Those who love you in an effort to support you end up saying negative and hateful things about your ex-spouse. And given that the ex-spouse is still a member of the body of Christ, it breeds enmity and hate within the body.

The rest of the world and especially the church condemns you by defining your home as 'broken', and describing your situation as permanently sinful. In so doing they also pile hate upon you. It therefore makes it very difficult to emerge on the other side of a divorce with any kind of positive light. And if one does emerge safely on the other side, it is very difficult to ever trust or love the church again, given how pharisaic and unforgiving the body of Christ can be.

I give God and God alone the credit for using my divorce

as the catalyst to propel me into Ministry. I have come to believe that it is indeed true that all things work together for good to them that love God, to them who are called according to His purpose. However, Scripture does not say that all things work *easily* for that good. And it was not easy for me.

I was unemployed and petrified that I would not be able to give Oduma as good a life and an education as I had been given by my parents. I was frightened about facing the church and society and having to deal with the stigma of divorce. My mother discouraged me from continuing with the contentiousness with Seth and so in one of my lucid days, I decided to let everything go and not contend with him over anything that was supposed to accrue to me as part of the divorce.

I even promised God that if any of what was due me was ever given to me, I would give it all to His church. I also decided that I was not going to go back to the USA as a single parent. I was going to start afresh in Ghana. I was determined that I would make it against all odds. I did not know how or in what form this fresh start would take but that was my decision.

The best way I can describe my life at that time was like the man Jesus spoke about who was walking down from Jerusalem to Jericho, when he was struck down by robbers and left for dead lying on the side of the road. The walk from Jerusalem to Jericho itself was not the problem. Many people went down that road. That road is just like marriage, and many people go down that road. But not everyone winds up attacked by fear and unfaithfulness that leave them broken and lying helpless on the side of the road.

But ironically, it was only because the man was lying on the side of the road that his salvation came along in the form of the Good Samaritan. If he hadn't been attacked, he would have continued walking, feeling strong and capable and would certainly not have accepted a ride on a stranger's donkey. In other words, the trigger to his salvation was his downfall. The trigger to my salvation was my divorce. If I had stayed married, it's possible that I might never have had the silence in my head to hear God when He spoke to me. Who knows!

GOOD SAMARITANS

During that time, just like the man in the parable, there were many who walked by me on the other side of the road, not wanting to be associated with the stink of my divorce. Unfortunately, many of them are known 'people of God' in our society, who in an effort to uphold the statutes of Scripture neglected to show love and compassion. But there were also many good Samaritans, normal everyday people who were not renowned 'men of God,' yet they in various ways, lifted me up and put me on their donkey and carried me to a place of healing.

One of them was my cousin Michael. I had met Michael once when I was fifteen and he was twenty-three. He lived in Kumasi, a city about two hundred kilometers north of Accra, which is how come we had never met. My parents had taken my brother and me up to Kumasi to meet my mum's half-sister. Apparently, she was a very wealthy woman and I was keen to meet her. She was bubbly and chatty but lived in an apartment which struck me as odd until I realized she owned the whole apartment block. She had a whole bunch of kids and other young people who were related to her in various ways and one of them was Michael. Michael was like a mother hen. Not physically. In fact, he was very tall and quite slim, but he had a brooding personality.

He made it his job to take care of everyone else. He organized our days, decided what we would do, where we would go, what sites were best for us to see, what food was best. And he was so completely oblivious to everyone else's objection to his suggestions that after a while we just stopped objecting. We all just went along with Michael because there really wasn't any other option.

Eighteen years later, that domineering personality was exactly what I needed. Michael just showed up at my mum's house in the middle of my crisis. He said he was working on moving to Australia to join his wife. After one afternoon of listening to my plight, he took over my life just like he had taken over all of ours when we first met him. He was furious about my situation and just cursed at everyone and everything that he determined was causing me pain. He reminded me very much of Captain Haddock in the comic book Tintin, yelling "blistering barnacles" at the wind if it blew in the wrong direction. It didn't matter what or who it was, Michael would get mad and defend me like his life depended on it.

I told Michael I'd always wanted to start my own company but I was frightened because I had no financial back-up. He jumped all over it and encouraged me to go for it. Together he and I examined what I had done with my life so far. I had an Engineering degree, an MBA with a focus on Procurement and I had worked as an Engineer and as a Procurement Manager in Human Resource (HR) services. In the HR field, I had been working on the Procurement side of HR focused on what HR firms need. After analyzing my work experience and the Ghanaian terrain, we decided that it would be best if I did something in the area of HR. We named the resultant company after my mother. Within a month of this discussion, Michael found me an office, got me two desks and chairs and offered himself as employee number one for a pittance! We took a loan from my mum and started with Corporate training, CV development, interview skills development and attempted to grow from there. That was how I started up my consulting firm. At the time we made very little money but I was just glad to have something take my mind off all my troubles.

Over time, we got business contracts from a few companies and we tried our best to make some real money. As time went on however, the fact that the work we did was so time consuming took a toll on the company and it failed to thrive. I would occasionally pray to God to help turn around the fortunes of the company but my prayers seemed to have fallen on deaf ears as things got worse for us. But, it didn't matter too much then, Michael and his endless encouragement and belief in my ability was all I needed.

Alongside Michael, I had Serwah who gave me a listening ear. She and I met when she came to sixth-form at GIS. I was in Form-Four and I'm not quite sure how we became friends, I only remember that we could talk about anything and she was like a big sister to me. While I was away in the USA, for over ten years, we never spoke, but the day I returned to Ghana, I called her and we picked up the conversation right where we left off in secondary school. She became the person to whom I would turn to when I needed a listening ear. Despite how down I was, she always managed to make me laugh about my situation. Looking back now, that was the best thing that could have happened for me then, the ability to laugh even when my world was crumbling around me.

Then there was Margaret Bartels. She was my History teacher when I was fourteen. In fact, she was the teacher who reviewed Brian's essay and with his permission, gave it to me to read. She had taken a liking to me in school and we remain friends to this day. When I came home for maternity leave, she sensed very quickly that something wasn't quite right with my marriage. But she never asked.

The day I told her that my marriage was a total mess, all she said was, "I know." I'm not quite sure how she knew but I guessed that when you've lived up to a certain point, you just know these things. What she did next was not to lecture me or even to pry, she simply asked that I come to her class to speak to her students who were getting ready to leave for university. I guess she just wanted me to take my mind off my problems.

Not being that far removed from being a university student myself, I obliged. That day was when I discovered that talking to young people is a thing I enjoy doing. That evening we had an open conversation. I talked mostly. And like a truly good friend, she just listened and said she would support whatever I decided. She is still probably my most sound and balanced counsel to date.

Reverend Ekow Acquah was introduced to me just before I got married. My mother, feeling very unhappy with my choice of spouse had asked him to pray for me. I am very skeptical of people who 'pray' for people but when he and I got to talk, he turned out to be very level-headed. Naturally, when my marriage started crumbling, he was called back in to pray some more. By then, he and I had become quite good friends and whenever we would talk he assured me that God would lift me out of all that I was going through and use me for His purpose.

The "lift me out" part I found comforting but the "using me" part I could not fathom. So I didn't. He never used the word priest but he kept saying, "God will use you." With all my problems at the time the thing I was least interested in, was being used by a God under whose hand I was currently perishing.

Next was Reverend Ekow Idan. At some point in my struggle with the shame of divorce and my life in general, I started attending several different churches in search of God. I was all over the place, from the most conservative Catholic Church to the loudest Charismatic Church. I tried them all looking for a God who would have mercy on me. One day, I attended a prayer meeting at a church on the outskirts of Accra. It was an afternoon of praise and worship and I had hoped that somewhere in there God would show up. But He did not. Well, not the way I was hoping He would. In all honesty, I am not quite sure what that would have been. What happened instead was that the ushers at this event led a well-dressed gentleman to my row. He and I nodded politely at each other and then he sat in the seat next to mine.

At some point during the program, the MC called on the next speaker and up stood my neighbor. He went and spoke. He had a bit of an affected American accent but he was well-spoken. He spoke briefly and returned to his seat. I shook his hand when he returned and that's what began what has turned out to be a good friendship to date. He introduced himself as Reverend Ekow Idan. We exchanged numbers and he promised to keep in touch.

About two weeks later, he called. We must have talked for about two hours. He was so easy to talk to and something in me felt very safe with him. I shared with him my struggles in life and in particular with God. And he was incredibly encouraging with each of our conversations ending with him praying for me over the phone. After one of our marathon phone calls, he said to me that God had revealed to him that I was going to be a priest. At the time, I thought it was utter nonsense. So in as much as I loved talking to him, I dismissed all his priestly prophecies about my life.

Father Daniel Tettedji, my last good Samaritan, was

introduced to me by Serwah while I was in the throes of my divorce. He was a young Catholic priest, about my age, who had provided her a lot of comfort and encouragement when she was going through a difficult time. As a Catholic priest I was concerned that he would condemn me to hell once he heard I was going through a divorce. But I couldn't have been more wrong.

We met in his office in downtown Osu and all he did was listen. I don't recall that he actually gave me any advice but I found that listening ear extremely soothing. Overtime we became friends. I continue to go to him for "listening" whenever I have any issue.

One day, I was driving to my struggling business, when I was suddenly overcome with a deep sense of regret for all the escapades of my past. I felt this desperate need to get everything off my chest and verbally confess my sins to someone. Padre, as I call Father Daniel, was the only person I could trust. So I called him crying,

"Where are you? I must see you now!"

"I'm not in Accra, I'm at our retreat center in Kordiabe." He replied sounding very concerned. "Can you come here? It's on the Michel Camp-Akosombo road."

I knew the general direction of Michel Camp but I didn't know where the retreat center was.

"I'm coming Padre. I'll call you when I get to Michel Camp."

How I made the forty-five-minute drive to the retreat center without wrecking my car is a mystery and a miracle to me. Because, for the entire drive I was blinded by tears and I had this writhing pain in my chest.

When I saw Padre I embraced him and just cried on his shoulder. I wonder now what was going through his head. I was crying so intensely, that he must have thought I had killed someone.

Eventually, I settled down and we sat and talked. Well, I talked, for at least an hour, about all the sins I had indulged in since I was a teenager. My last statement to him was, "So what is my penance? I know you Catholics require some kind of penance before God will forgive me." His answer still touches me till today. He said, "A broken and contrite heart, God will not despise." (Psalm 51:17). He prayed with me and that was it. I felt like the weight of the world had been lifted off my shoulders. God still had a lot of work to do on me but I often joke with Him, God that is, that while Paul may have had the 'road to Damascus' I have the 'road to Michel Camp'.

All these people; Michael, Serwah, Margaret, Ekow Acquah, Ekow Idan, and Father Daniel played critical roles in keeping me sane during that phase of my life. They each helped in my journey to the inn of healing described in the parable of the Good Samaritan. The inn where through each of their efforts, I found hope. I don't know where I would be now without them and I thank God for making them available to me at that crucial time in my life. But, I still didn't have what I needed. What I ultimately needed was a healing for my soul. Something only God could do.

> **I am the vine; you are the branches. If you remain in me and I in you, you will bear much fruit; apart from me you can do nothing. John 15:5 (NIV)**

WHAT IS SUCCESS?

As I tried to settle down in Ghana and make the best of my life, I constantly juxtaposed my prevailing situation to my previous status in life. I used to have a great job. I used to be a Design Engineer and then a Procurement Manager at Cummins. I worked hard and was extremely dynamic. I was one of very few black women engineers at Cummins. I was so active in the company and the community that I won the 2009 "20-Under-40" Entrepreneurship award in Columbus Indiana, earning me a spot in the local newspapers. I had sat as a Commissioner on the Human Rights Commission in Columbus, Indiana. A position that was handed to me because of my demonstrated hard work, as well as being a Black-African Woman Engineer.

I owned a BMW, which opened the eyes of my brother to the concept of a BMW as opposed to an Audi. He still drives one today; forever altered by my 'wisdom.' I lived for his approval and so for him to imitate me was the ultimate. I used to own a large home which I decorated with modern furniture and unique art pieces from my various travels. My friends liked coming to see my home because of the way it was decorated. And I reveled in their approval.

The truth is, my life in those days looked wonderful on the outside. But I was dying inside.

In those days I loved traveling, especially by road. The open spaces made me feel free and gave me hope that maybe I'd find what would fill my emptiness if I just 'went into the space'. Whenever I had the time, I'd just take off in some direction. Just so I could have a long solitary drive on an open highway. Once, I drove from Indiana to Florida, roughly fifteen hours, to watch a rocket launch. Unfortunately, there was bad weather, so the launch was cancelled. Another time, I was watching a basketball game featuring San Antonio. The commentator at some point said San Antonio was a beautiful city. The next day, I bought gas and drove for over two thousand kilometers to San Antonio. It is indeed a beautiful city. But the reality is that it didn't give me the satisfaction I needed. It didn't fill the deep void I felt.

When I compared my life then, where I had everything and my life now where I had nothing, the feeling of misery and emptiness was the same. Clearly, personal belongings and status was not the answer. So what was? My inability to properly answer that question and contextualize what it means to be successful, was why I was in this state. First of all, I thought being successful meant having nice material things. And I thought having nice material things would lead to happiness and fulfilment. When that proved incorrect, I decided that marriage was an essential part of success and thus a panacea to happiness. So I got married, only to realize that was also not an answer to the void in me. Now I was 'broke', single, unemployed and still unhappy.

What was missing was God.

> **But seek first his kingdom and his righteousness and all these things will be given to you as well. Matthew 6:33 (NIV)**

HITTING ROCK BOTTOM

Within a few months, Michael moved to Australia and the company continued to struggle and had practically collapsed. So here I was with my thirty-seven-year-old life in shambles. I was divorced, living with my mother, running a failing company that had left me so broke that it was my retired mother who supported me by giving me the equivalent of $100 a month. That was the worst part for me. The fact that I needed that money and literally could not survive without it. By God's grace, my daughter was too young to be aware of my plight. To add to my shame, my mother was fully funding Oduma's Daycare fees, her food and everything. So in as much as I didn't have to worry about how my child would eat, I was deeply distressed, not to mention embarrassed, that I could not provide for her.

I made no contribution towards the household because I just couldn't. I had been living with my mum for three years now and I remember after the first year, I was furious because my brother called and asked me how much longer I was planning to 'freeload' on our mother. I vowed that day to be out of her house by the end of the year. And yet two years later, I was still there. Being a burden. Every attempt I had made to turn things around, just fell flat. Clearly, something was not right.

My woes came to a head when I received a letter from GIS accepting my daughter into the school. This was a dream I had nurtured since I was eighteen, that my unborn child would someday attend my alma mater. And now here I was nineteen years later, holding a letter in my hand that said my daughter had been accepted into GIS. Yet all I could feel was fear and disappointment in myself. The problem was that I needed to make a deposit of four thousand dollars to hold her place in the school. I simply did not have that money. I was literally living on a $100 food stamp. Where on earth was I going to find four thousand dollars? I could literally see my nineteen-year dream slip through my fingers. And it made me miserable. I called Margaret who had just lost her husband and between our two woes we cried bitterly.

That night I called my brother. Given his previous commentary about me, what he said to me surprised me. He said, "I don't know how you will do it but I know you. You'll find a way to make it work." That statement went through my body like an adrenaline shot. It stirred up something in me and made me believe in myself. It told me that he had confidence in me. And it told me that I really needed to get up and move because at least one person believed in me. It made me see that my resurrection, my salvation, my ability to make it was inside me and only me. No one else could save me except He that is in me. That feeling and those thoughts were and are still the thoughts I use to get myself going whenever I feel stuck.

Prior to that, everything in my world revolved around fear. I spent countless hours in bed too frightened to do much more than feed my child. I didn't realize it then and nobody recognized it but I was struggling with depression. All I remember was that there was a lot of darkness and heaviness in my head. There were no signs that things would get any better. But that night, I thought long and hard about what my brother said and some things dawned on me. To start with, I had no reason to be unemployed because I was well educated. Secondly, though I was divorced, I was neither dead nor condemned and therefore I had a responsibility to live. Thirdly, I was going through a custody battle for my daughter and so what I needed to do was to ensure that I could give her the quality of life she deserved, otherwise, I could lose her. Empowered by these, I mustered enough courage and started to try to turn things around.

SOMETHING IS JUST NOT RIGHT

It was right around this time that I met a lady called Angela. Like Ambily, she had what appeared to be a very deep spirituality. Unlike Ambily though, she focused a lot on the dangers of evil spirits. But still I was drawn to her. I admired what I perceived to be her close relationship with God. And since I had also started making efforts to get closer to God, again, we naturally spent a lot time talking about God. Of course, my friendship with Ambily and her subsequent introduction of Jesus to me had given me a fair idea of what it meant to have God at the center of everything one does. So even though I had lost that close relationship I developed with Jesus, somewhere deep inside me, I guess I yearned for Him.

> **As the deer pants for streams of water, so my soul pants for you, my God. Psalm 42:1 (NIV)**

One day, I shared with Angela the woes of my company. She advised me to venture into the importation of goods, which was her line of business. It seemed like a good idea so I agreed to it. I had never traded in anything before, so I leaned very heavily on her expertise. Upon her advice, I took my very last ditch money, my 401K (retirement fund) and with that move I literally put my life in her hands. Right there was my mistake; leaning on another person for my salvation. I was convinced that with her guidance I was on my way to financial independence. And because she seemed so close to God, I never bothered to check-in with Him myself.

We often presume that every seemingly good thing comes from God, especially when the people who present it to us talk about God a lot. Today, I would have prayed to God and waited for His clear instructions before entering into that venture. But that was not what I did. I did not seek God's approval. I just followed Angela's advice and took a dive into 'buying-and-selling' with my would-be retirement money.

I converted the office of my failed business into a wholesale shop and paid one more year of rent, and overnight became a business woman. Again, things went well in the beginning. I was able to make enough money to import my own containers of goods. I even signed a ninety-day payment free agreement with a Turkish company where my company had the sole rights to their products in Ghana. I was on a roll and as I did better and better in my business, I talked to God less and less. I pushed Him into the background. While Angela on the other hand was very much in the foreground. After all, she was the one making a real difference. She was the one making sure I had an income. That was when God stepped in and messed it all up for me.

I have come to understand that when God says He's a jealous God, He means it literally. He will take all His toys out of our pram the moment He sees that we value the toys more than Him. And that is what happened to me. First of all, the local currency, the Ghana Cedi, took a sudden and very drastic dip. Since I was buying my imported goods in dollars and selling them in Ghana Cedis, my net worth plummeted overnight. When I did the math, I realized that even if I sold the goods I had twice over, I would still be in debt.

> **Do not worship any other god, for the Lord, whose name is Jealous, is a jealous God. Exodus 34:14 (NIV)**

I remembered at the time that a couple of years earlier, Seth had said to me that without him, I would never succeed in life. Between that and the constant commentary from Angela about the works of the devil and witchcraft, I started to believe that I was cursed. And my fear intensified. I quickly turned back to God to seek solace and answers in Him. But nothing happened. Meanwhile, Angela would always remind me that the only way the devil would not get me was if I gave every aspect of my life to God.

I heard her but I was too consumed with fear to act. I drove a BMW at the time, the last remnant of my past life, so I decided that as my last proper 'asset,' I would sell it, buy a cheaper car and offset my debt. I knew a car dealer called Ofori, who was a friend of my cousin Michael. I approached him like a big brother and in trust, I gave him my car to sell. Paperwork and everything. He sold the car and pocketed the money. So now, not only was

I still in debt, I was also without a car. I was mortified and I felt very stupid. Again, my mother, the good Samaritan, saved me by lending me her Suzuki, which she kept as a spare car in case of emergency.

THE POWER OF SIMPLE PRAYERS

In my frustration, I went down on my knees and in tears told God that I surrender my entire life to Him to do as He pleased. I asked Him to take charge. I don't believe I prayed for more than a few minutes. My prayer was simply this, "Dear God, I don't seem to be able to manage my life, so You take over. I hand every aspect of it over to You." And with that simple prayer, everything went haywire.

The next container I had on the high seas was dropped at the port and every single thing in it broke and spilled. My insurance wasn't enough to cover the damages and so I lost my entire order. I was forced to take a loan from a loan shark since the banks in Ghana require ridiculous collateral. The interest on the only loan available to me was 50%. Needless to say the business never recovered from it. I failed again.

I was so disappointed in God. How could He do this to me? The idea was for Him to improve things, not destroy everything. But this time I was resolved to surrendering everything to God no matter what. I had tried life on my own on so many different occasions and in so many different ways that, whilst I did not know what lay ahead, there was no way I was going to go back to trying to run my own life.

Meanwhile, Angela kept telling me to pray and break the curse that was on my life. It was very overwhelming for me and I spent hours and hours just talking very plainly to God. I would pace up and down in my mother's garden at all times of the day and night, wanting to hear or see something from God. I wasn't sure what I wanted but I knew I needed something. I would yell at Him, praise Him, cry to Him. I was so desperate. Desperate for God to save me from the devils and witches who Angela said were out to get me. And who, from all indications, seemed to be succeeding.

But through it all God was silent. I felt like giving up and turning my back completely on Him. But something in me burned with anger at God. I wanted an answer from Him. I was not willing to let Him destroy my life and get away with it. I was determined to harass Him and force Him to address my plight and explain Himself, even if it killed me. Day in and day out I prayed, asking for answers to why my life was going the way it was. Then, one day, an answer came through a very unlikely source.

I have an African-American friend called Darnell Hardy who is a flight attendant. Whenever he was part of the crew into Ghana, he and I would meet and talk about everything and anything including God. One day, he called me from the USA, which was very unusual.

He said, "I have a message for you from God."

"Really?" I said feeling frightened. Here I was demanding answers and yet when it came I was scared.

"Yeah, I don't know why but for the past few days I keep getting the same Scripture in my head and God says it's for you."

"Hmmmm. OK, what is it?"

"Its Matthew 6:33, "seek first his kingdom and his righteousness and all these things will be given to you as well.""

"Right. Soooo what does that mean?"

"I think He means seek His heart first and He will give you

everything in His hands," Darnell answered.

SEEK YE FIRST THE KINGDOM OF GOD

I must say, I was very disappointed. Because I was expecting or rather hoping for something like Jeremiah 29:11, "'For I know the plans I have for you,' declares the Lord, 'plans to prosper you and not to harm you, plans to give you hope and a future.'" That in my view would have been a far more appropriate and meaningful message than "Seek ye first…" What on earth was I supposed to do with that!?

When I told Angela, her interpretation was that the Anglican church is a 'spiritist' church that worships dead people, as in saints. And that as long as I was part of that church, I would not have a "good covering." She explained to me that this was why it was so easy for the devil to get to me. So essentially, God was asking me to find a church that has His presence.

That is what led me to the hunt for God in different churches. Church hopping in an effort to seek and hopefully find this kingdom of God. But all I found was further confusion. Each church had its own view of God and why bad things were happening to me and why bad things happen to people in general. Some churches said I needed to sow a seed, so I did with the little I had. Some said I needed to make an atonement for sin. A financial atonement to be precise. So I did. Some said to just pray. I was praying and nothing was happening. The more churches I went to, the more broke and more frustrated I got.

Today, many people have been deceived into believing that their salvation is in a particular church or in a particular pastor, priest or prophet. So we allow them to prey on our pain, ignorance and desperation and use it to siphon our money all in the name of prosperity. And the reason we fall victim is because we don't know our Scripture. For many of us, the pastor, priest, prophet and the denomination of church have become our salvation and not Christ. And so we go to church and we recite creeds that we've never bothered to think about. Or we shout and bang cymbals without really understanding why. And at the end of the day we leave church feeling saved. But what we're feeling is really just adrenaline.

I was blown away the day I read in Acts 17:11 that the people of Berea after listening to Paul actually went back to examine Scripture to make sure that what Paul had said was true. And the best part is that the Bible didn't condemn them as unbelievers for not just taking Paul at his word. They were described as "open-minded." In other words, they were thinkers, who were willing to take responsibility for their own salvation.

> **The people of Berea were more open-minded than the people of Thessalonica. They were very willing to receive God's message and every day they carefully examined the Scriptures to see if what Paul said was true. Acts 17:11 (NIV)**

All the churches I had attended made me see that there is no one perfect church. Some churches are somber, some are loud, some cater for young families, others cater for the elderly, some have choirs that sing like angels and others have live bands that make it seem like you're at a concert. But all of that is unimportant if the true and full gospel of Jesus Christ is not being preached or is compromised in any way. That should be our primary determinant for attending any church. Everything else, the rituals, the lights, the cuteness of the girls or boys who attend the church, is secondary and should never be the sole basis upon which we choose a church. Frustrated with it all, I reported all my findings to Angela, who then said, "Why don't you tell God you want to get to know Him."

That night, I went for my usual late night run. It had become my habit to pray while I run. So I prayed the same prayer over and over again, "God I want to know You, God I want to know You." It was during that run that I heard Him clear as day say, "If you want to know Me, study Me."

"Study You? Like how? Like academically?"

"Yes, 'like academically.'"

Right there and then, I stopped mid-run, turned around and went back home to research seminaries and Bible schools. I was excited about the prospect of going to a school to figure out what God's deal was. But I was also being very cautious because the only people I knew who went to these institutions were priests and I did not want to become a priest.

My research led me to three institutions, one was Pentecostal, the second Charismatic and the third an Orthodox seminary. In my view, the Orthodox seminary was completely out because I was convinced that if I went there, I would be brainwashed into becoming a priest. So I inquired about the Charismatic Bible School but they only had weekend classes, all day Saturday and half the day on Sunday. With a young child, there was no way I was going to pull that off. I honestly don't recall what it was with the Pentecostal Bible School but they also had some condition that made it impossible for me to attend.

That left me with the very Orthodox Trinity Theological Seminary. And for me that was out of the question. So I abandoned the idea all together and decided to just pray and read my Bible. That was when God decided to become chatty. He began to press me about attending Trinity. Everywhere I turned,

I saw, or heard, or thought about something that had to do with that seminary. Whenever I prayed, my heart was heavy, as if I was doing something wrong.

One day, I was driving past the seminary and I kept having the same recurring thought, *just go in there!* I had actually driven past the seminary's gate when I started to get a stress headache from this thought. Wanting to get God out of my head, I made a U-turn and drove to the administration block of the seminary. As I was walking through the doors, a very distinguished-looking priest was walking out. He smiled very warmly and said to me, "You are not a student here."

"No sir, I'm not," I responded.

"How may I help you? I'm the Dean."

"Oh ok. Well, I'm looking for information about the programs you have here."

He turned and walked with me into the lobby and pulled out a bunch of pamphlets that spoke about the programs they offered. They ranged from certificate programs, to PhDs. I said to him very bluntly, "Well I'm not a priest and I never want to be a priest. I just want to get to know God better. Do you have a program for people who want to know God better but don't want to be priests?"

He seemed amused and said, "Yes we do, it's called a Master of Arts in Ministry, the next degree program starts in April."

Fifteen minutes later, I was back in my car with a full application packet on the passenger seat and a world of relief in my heart. I could literally feel God smiling. My new problem was how my mother was going to respond when I told her.

Surprisingly, she was over the moon. She thought it was my best move in the last three years and made it her job to get me all the necessary endorsements and even offered to pay half my school fees. I was completely blown away. So in my excitement, I went and told Angela.

She blew her top! And told me I was wasting my time pursuing religion and not money. She reminded me of how I had nothing and that I was going to waste my life. Her reaction was so spontaneous and so contrary to her claim of closeness to God. It was actually really strange. She was so upset about it that she told her husband who asked me the next day with great disdain what I hoped to accomplish with all my education. It was as if by pursuing God in this way, I had somehow offended them. I was so stunned and quite frankly, frightened that I pulled back from them and eventually ended the friendship.

> **For such men are false apostles, deceitful workers, masquerading as apostles of Christ. And no wonder, for Satan himself masquerades as an angel of light. 2 Corinthians 11:14 (NIV)**

By the end of the week, my mother had completed my application form with endorsements, legal stamps and everything. I took it back to the nice Dean and was scheduled for an interview. That week, Darnell came to Ghana and had another message for me. This time it wasn't a Bible verse. He simply said, "God said to tell you that your life is like a field and everything that has been planted on the field up until now is not from Him. So He is clearing the field and once He is done, He will plant new seed and in time, it will grow and it will be beautiful." I honestly did not know what to make of this message either but it sounded far more promising than, "Seek ye first…"!

Shortly after that, Darnell stopped flying to Ghana and we didn't stay in touch as much. But recently, I was interviewed on a show called "The Executive Lounge" and whilst the video was doing its rounds on social media, Darnell sent me a message on Facebook and asked if I remembered the messages he brought to me all those years ago. How could I forget? I replied. We sent laughing and praying hand emoticons to each other. God is indeed faithful to His words!

Meanwhile, my challenges continued. I was unemployed and very broke but eager to learn about God. Unfortunately, my motivation to learn about God was still very negative. I was angry with Him for 'messing up my life'. Deep within me I felt as if He had betrayed the eight-year-old me by allowing all these negative things to happen. I wanted Him to love me and make things better for me. But I also wanted Him to suffer. I wanted to hurt Him, by studying Him and then walking away, just so He could feel the same abandonment and hurt that I felt!!

CHAPTER SEVEN

CALLING, CALLING...CALLED

But Moses said, "Pardon your servant, Lord. Please send someone else."
Exodus 4:13 (NIV)

SEMINARY

It was far more complicated to get into seminary than I thought. I didn't realize people actually wanted to go to seminary. I had assumed it was free admission as long as you could afford the fees. But it was not so at all. Many people annually are rejected just like any other institution. It turned out that to get into seminary, apart from the application forms, there was a written exam and an oral exam. You only got in if you passed the former and were deemed fit after the latter.

This was the first time I felt nervous about the process. I had been arrogant and indignant throughout. Eager to prove to my would-be professors that the whole God thing is a hoax. And now, I needed to take an exam? In all honesty, apart from John 3:16 and the Lord's Prayer which I knew was somewhere in the Bible, all my church experience hadn't taught me much about the Bible or Christianity. I suddenly felt very unqualified and ill prepared for my exam and my interview. But I was in the room, so all I could do was proceed with the knowledge I had.

The exam consisted of two questions. The first question was, "In the two creation accounts, what was the cause and the effect of the fall?" I had no idea there were two creation accounts! The second question was, "What is the Kingdom of God?" Now, even though I didn't know there were two creation stories, I was aware of the fall. But as for the kingdom of God, I simply had no idea what it was. Fortunately, I only needed to answer one question. So I decided to answer the former.

Forty-five minutes later, I put my pen down and went to the waiting room for the oral exam. There were almost one hundred of us interviewing that day. I really had no idea seminary was so popular. I waited for about an hour, sitting next to a gentleman called Captain. Well that was his title and not his name. He was ex-military and we ended up talking for the duration of the wait. In seminary we became good friends and a few years later we worked together.

Eventually, I was called in. I walked into a cold stark room. And there in front of me, sitting quite some distance from the door, behind a long desk were three intelligent looking men. It turns out that they were professors at the Seminary. It felt as though part of the exam was for them to watch how I did my perp-walk to the single chair in the middle of the room facing them. None of them said anything till I got to the chair. I stood beside the chair and after an awkward silence, I sat. It was then that they asked my name. I told them and then they asked which of the two essay questions I answered. "The fall" I answered. Then one professor said, "Good, then tell us the answer to the Kingdom of God question." *Really?* My first thought was to blurt out that if I knew the answer to the question, I would have answered that one. But at the time, that didn't seem like wisdom. So I quietly said, "I really don't know what the Kingdom of God is."

"Try, just tell us something." was the response from the panel.

I said what I now know was a whole lot of total rubbish. I hoped it made more sense to them than it did to me. It must have, because a month later, I received my admission letter. Or maybe it was such gibberish that they realized how desperately I needed the education of a seminary, hence the admission. Either way, I was in and now I could determine once and for all, if I was going to keep pursuing God or just move on.

> **Ask and it will be given to you; seek and you will find; knock and it will be opened to you. For everyone who asks receives and he who seeks finds and to him who knocks it will be opened. Matthew 7:7-8 (NIV)**

Right after Easter 2011, seminary started. On the first day of lectures, I realized I was probably the most unholy person in the class. We were a class of about sixty people; and everybody, apart from one gentleman and me, were leaders or priests in their respective churches. I, on the other hand, was just a dues-paying member of my church, technically, since it was my mother who was actually paying on my behalf.

Since all my church hopping had yielded nothing, I went back to the Anglican Church, because at least there I could have communion. But certainly I was not going to pay annual dues to an institution whose sole value addition to me was a sliver of bread and a sip of wine. In fact, it was my regular practice to only sit momentarily after communion, just spending enough time to make it look like I had said a short prayer and then I would walk right out of church.

Once seminary started, I found I enjoyed it. Whenever I was in class, I felt the same peace I felt when I was in the Cathedral all those years ago in secondary school. I felt calm and I felt like I belonged. I enjoyed the praise and worship we would do as students before class and I left every class feeling extremely fulfilled. There was a particular professor who would end every lecture with a hymn. He somehow always managed to find a hymn that was relevant to what he had just taught us. That made a huge impression on me and it has become a style I adopt regularly when I deliver sermons now as a priest. That man, Professor Hilliard Dogbe, eventually became my thesis advisor.

> **You, however, continue in the things you have learned and become convinced of, knowing from whom you have learned them. 2 Timothy 3:14 (NASB)**

DISCOVERING MY GIFT

Our first module was the Old Testament. Apart from the children's Bible that I had read cover to cover several times as a child, I knew nothing about the Old Testament. The history, stories and the various details about the people described in the Old Testament fascinated me. But more than that, I discovered I had a knack for understanding Scripture and making it relatable. I found that when I would read the Bible, the images and the meanings of the Scriptures would jump out at me like a children's 3D novel. It was so real that sometimes, it frightened me because I was so convicted about how I understood the Scriptures but I often had no way of proving or backing what was going on in my head.

I had in the past been such a critic of people who say the "Holy Spirit told them something or other," but all of a sudden, here I was, experiencing such insight into Scripture that I didn't need a prophet to tell me this was not my own wisdom. Clearly, something, or rather Someone, was giving me these insights. It was God Himself.

It is abundantly clear to me now that, the Bible gift I received as an eight-year-old child, was part of God's grand plan for me. I believe it was that illustrated children's Bible that kindled my imagination and set the stage for how I understood Scripture whilst I was in seminary and indeed how I understand the Scriptures now as a priest. I have come to believe that this gift I have for appreciating and teaching Scripture in such simple terms is part of my calling. To help make God and the Bible relatable to other people.

> **The unfolding of your words gives light; it gives understanding to the simple. Psalm 119:130 (NIV)**

GOD DOES NOT GIVE US BURDENS WE CAN'T CARRY

At this point, both my HR company and my shop were struggling so badly that I spent most of my days in the office just reading my lecture notes and preparing for my evening lectures. I used seminary to drown out my woes. Whenever I took my thoughts off the things of God, I felt deeply miserable and ashamed. So, I focused on seminary and tried to figure out who God really is and more importantly, who I am to God. And whether I should even bother with Him anymore, given how badly my life had turned out.

God didn't help the situation either. Everything in my life kept slipping from bad to worse. With both of my businesses failed, my only income was still this measly but much appreciated allowance of roughly $100 from my mother. My life was a failure, at least per human standard. Yet, I had this joy in my heart that was very hard for me to explain at the time. I thought the joy was because I had a new exciting thing to focus on, as in getting a theological degree. But later, I came to understand that, what I was experiencing was what I had often heard rattled off meaninglessly as the peace of God that surpasses all understanding.

> **And the peace of God, which transcends all understanding, will guard your hearts and your minds in Christ Jesus. Philippians 4:7 (NIV)**

Seminary was grueling but I excelled. After two years, I graduated as the only woman with a distinction that year. As the time for graduation drew close, I started to panic because I didn't know what I was going to do with myself after school. For what it was worth, now I was an unemployed seminarian. Without seminary, I would just be unemployed!

At this point, God and I had become civil friends. I believe we had a healthy respect for each other, although there was still a bit of suspicion, at least on my part. I knew He loved me unconditionally but I wondered whether He understood me and my world enough to take the necessary steps to make sure I was successful. The failure of my businesses and my marriage were proof that there was a disjoint between God and myself. All the same, I trusted Him enough to ask basic questions and put in a few simple prayer requests.

One day, in bed, I prayed and asked God to guide my next steps, and show me what to do next. And right on cue, in typical God style, He started to do things which honestly at the time felt like punishment. Now I know that God weaves His plans for us so masterfully, that even the worst things are for the best outcomes.

One such God move happened on a Sunday, when I, unlike other Sundays, had decided to sit in church long enough to listen to the announcements. Well, I wasn't actually listening but I was conscious enough to hear my priest, Reverend Canon Samuel

Lamptey, announce that moving forward, the two seminarians in the church would have to start preaching. My ears perked up and I remember my heart dropping to the very pit of my stomach. I had always been a public speaker and I enjoyed speaking but this wasn't speaking. This was preaching! Preaching involves God's word. There was no way I was going to fudge my way through God's Word. Absolutely no way! God and I had enough issues, I wasn't willing to add this one to them!

But Canon Lamptey wasn't asking. He called me into his office after Mass and handed me the schedule for the month and there it was. My name. Scheduled for the Sunday after Easter. I spent a full month putting that sermon together. I think I re-read my entire set of books from my hermeneutics class to write this one sermon.

Finally, the Sunday after Easter arrived. I sat at the back of the church like I usually did next to my friend, Sam Eshun, may he rest in peace. I don't think I heard anything that was said that morning. I just kept checking my sermon and checking the order of service so I could keep track of how much time I had before I needed to preach. That morning was the first time I paid real attention to the order of the Anglican Mass. I had no idea it was so involving. I knew I was supposed to preach after the Gospel reading, so I kept ticking off the activities and nervously waited for it.

Eventually, the moment arrived, the Gospel was read and as the hymn after the Gospel was sung, Canon Lamptey stood up, nodded at me and started to move slowly towards the pulpit. I stood up and as I walked down the aisle from my seat at the back of the church, it dawned on me that my choice of seat was probably not the best. I could feel everyone's eyes on me, and as I approached the pew where my mother sat, towards the front of the church, I debated upon whether or not I should look at her. I decided against it. Finally, I made it to the pulpit and Canon Lamptey put his arm around my shoulder and explained to the church that I was going to preach that day. He was so relaxed about it. And that arm around my shoulder felt like God Himself conveying to me both comfort and strength.

It relaxed me. And the nervousness faded away. A bit. I said, "Let us pray" and with that, I started my first sermon which I called, 'On the Road to Emmaus'. After I got my first couple of sentences out, I felt like I had stepped outside of myself and this bold, outspoken person took over and was explaining Scripture in a way that I found absolutely fascinating. I remember listening to myself during the sermon and being amazed at the fact that it was me talking. I actually said things that I noted down as aspects of the sermon that I should remember and apply to my life. It was a complete out of body experience and when it was over, the applause jolted me back into myself and I felt small again.

> **Do not worry about what to say or how to say it. At that time, you will be given what to say. Matthew 10:19 (NIV)**

It was incredible. Here I was, with one little degree in Theology, preaching in front of several great minds like the late Professor John S. Pobee, one of the foremost theologians in Africa. Somehow, I had successfully delivered a sermon that clearly resonated with the congregation. What struck me was that within the Anglican communion, clapping after a sermon is frowned upon because we believe that the deliverer of the sermon is fully inspired by God and therefore it is God who must be applauded and not the priest. But that day, everyone threw that belief out of the window and clapped cheerfully for me. That clapping has followed me to date. Each time I preach, the congregation claps. And I have taught myself to remind myself of the prayer I pray before each sermon which is this, "Dear God, let them see and hear You and not me." I am convinced that God truly answers that prayer and therefore all the clapping is really for Him and not me.

What happened that day was clearly the work of God. I imagine now that He must have laughed at me when I was so worried about delivering a sermon to the congregation. When God says, He does not give us burdens we cannot carry, it is real.

GOD CALLING‼

After Mass that morning, the whole church swarmed around me, full of congratulatory messages. And with that came the start of what I can only describe as my call into the priesthood. And a brand new torture under God's hand!

It began with endless chatter from various members of my church, St Anthony of Padua Anglican Church, about how I should become a priest. For two continuous years, every time I preached at church, this clapping would happen, several people would ask for a copy of my sermon, and a few people would call me aside and lecture me about how I needed to seriously consider becoming a priest. I know everyone just meant well but for me it was overwhelming.

I remember on one occasion, Reverend Ekow Acquah, the priest who my mum brought to pray for me before my wedding, asked me to come to his church and preach. As a Charismatic priest, he had started up his own church in Anomabo, a town about one hundred and fifty kilometers out of Accra. I had never preached outside of an Anglican church. Given that Charismatic priests tend to be extemporary preachers and I at the time didn't know how to preach extemporarily, I was uncertain about how I would be received. All the same, I decided to heed his call.

After I delivered my sermon that day, Reverend Acquah cried, because he says he could feel God speaking through me. After service that day, when we were leaving the church, the women in the congregation flocked around me. I was completely overwhelmed.

Not knowing what to do, I prayed. I was convinced my gift of public speaking was what had shrouded the eyes of people and given them the impression that I was called. So I prayed and asked God for discernment and for guidance. But He only made things worse. Not only did the pressure from people increase, I myself started to feel within me a yearning to serve Him in a greater capacity. It was the same yearning I had felt to go to Trinity Theological Seminary specifically, as opposed to any other school. I knew in my heart that if I became a priest, I would be doing something to make God happy. But I also felt it was too big an ask from God. I believed it to be unfair because I hadn't lived a life that was worthy of priesthood. I was convinced that a priest should have lived a life that was worthy of emulating. That certainly was not my life. And I didn't want to spend my priesthood defending my past. But God has assured us that we are new creatures in Him and all the shame of our past is erased and can never be held against us, not by the world and not by the church. But I was still stuck in self and worried about what people would say and think.

> **Do not be afraid; you will not be put to shame. Do not fear disgrace; you will not be humiliated. You will forget the shame of your youth. Isaiah 54:4 (NIV)**

Apart from all the wild partying in secondary school and university, I was divorced and I couldn't see how as a divorcee, I could legitimately represent a God who "hates divorce." And as many churches tried to get me to believe, hates divorcees as well. Secondly, I didn't think I could adjust my personality to become the morose, quiet, plain, holier-than-thou kind of person that priests are supposed to be. In addition to that, a part of me felt that it would appear as though I was becoming a priest because all else in my life had failed.

But God wouldn't let up. It seemed as if everywhere I turned, I saw something about priesthood. I heard it in songs, I saw it on billboards, it was just unrelenting. Thoughts of priesthood became such a large part of my everyday life that I started playing games with God, asking Him to show me signs of proof. In these games, what I would do was that, whenever I needed something, I'd say to God that if He answered my prayer, I'd become a priest.

I remember one day, in an effort to avoid traffic on the way to my daughter's school, I followed some taxi drivers and wound up getting lost. I drove around for a bit and then I recognized a road that would get me back on track as long as I took the correct left turn off that road. Unfortunately, there were about five left turns and I just didn't know which one to take. So I used this as an opportunity to play one of my 'God games'. I said to Him that if He showed me the correct turn, I'd become a priest. The prayer was barely over when I saw a building to my left with the words "God is Able" written boldly across the front of the house. The words were engraved in terrazzo and stretched about five feet across the top of the building. Immediately before this house was a left turn and I knew that was the correct turn. I took it. And indeed, it was the correct turn! I looked up to the heavens smiling and promptly told God that I was rescinding on this promise because it was too easy!

There was no way I was going to hinge the entire direction of my life on something Google Maps could have done for me. So I reneged on my end of the deal. And I told God that He needed to work harder to get me into priesthood. Over the next year, I made several of these deals with God and every single time, He came through. And every single time, I backed out.

Meanwhile, I continued to write and preach. I loved the process of putting a sermon together. It was like building a thing of beauty; the research, the language, the interspersion of hymns; I felt like I was creating something special for God and I believed it pleased Him. And each time even one person would say to me that my sermon had touched them, I could literally feel the heavens open up and pour out blessings on me. But when the preaching was done and the applause died down, the burden in my heart about priesthood would return. Between that and my poverty, I couldn't tell which was worse!

In my frustration, I reached out to Canon Lamptey, the originator of all my priestly woes. He was what we call a *worker priest* and worked as the Human Resources Director with the government's water company. A worker priest is a priest who has opted to work a full-time job in addition to being a priest. Another term that is often used is a *tent minister*, after Paul who in Acts 18:3 is described as a tent maker in addition to being…Paul.

So I booked an appointment with him to let him know how much I was struggling with this call. When I walked into his office, he welcomed me with a big hug and said immediately that we should pray. He said a short prayer and asked how he could help me. As I gathered my thoughts, I began to weep. That was the extent to which my call weighed on me. Till today, those memories still make me weep.

He held both my hands and said, "You can tell me anything."

"I don't want to be a priest!" I blurted out, "but God won't let me go. And I don't know what to do."

Between large drops of tears and several tissues, I relayed my story and my fears to him. As I spoke, I felt the burden in my heart ease. When I was done, there was a long silence. I watched him think. And I believed in my heart that he was going to give me some wisdom that would excuse me from priesthood.

But then he said, "I'm happy to hear you don't want to be a priest. It tells me you're truly called."

What!!

I was so stunned. All I could manage was to blink at him in silence. He then went on to explain to me that he had been praying about me for months and was certain in his heart that I was meant to be a priest. As far as he was concerned, everything I had said to him was confirmation of what he had heard from God. And in fact he had planned on discussing it with me. I felt betrayed. Canon Lamptey was supposed to be my salvation. And now, more than anyone, he was leading me to the 'slaughter'! In the end, he indeed was the priest who presented me to the Bishop as a candidate for priesthood.

After that conversation, I conceded. God had won.

He could have His priest. But not without one last deal.

RESPONDING TO GOD'S CALL

My financial situation still remained deeply troubling for myself and my family. My mother was footing the bill for my child's education and it became painfully clear to me that I needed to walk away from all my entrepreneurial attempts and just look for a job somewhere. So, in spite of myself, I made one last ditched effort to try and get out of priesthood. I made my final deal with God.

I prayed saying, "Dear God, I need a job. But I have too much experience to start from scratch. You know what I am capable of. So give me a job but here is the condition. I want to be in at the executive level in the company. You Lord can choose the industry. Amen." I promised Him that if He did this, I would become a priest. White flag. I ended this prayer by vowing to myself that I would not ask God about this again. With that, I drove to GIS to pick up my daughter.

That day was a Thursday.

I continued to go to my non-functioning business, primarily to get out of the house and write sermons. After all, I had paid the rent, so even if there was no revenue, it gave me a place of my own to sit. In those days, if I wasn't at my office, I was in the studio recording the Full Gospel Hour now called the Business Men's Voice - a radio ministry of the Full Gospel Business Men's Fellowship International. It airs on Citi 97.3 FM, in Accra.

How I got to be the host of that show itself was quite strange. My buddy Kofi Boateng was the host and I thought it was very cool. So one day I asked God if he could give me a cool gig like that. A few months later Kofi called and asked if I'd be willing to be his 'back-up' host for days when he couldn't make the show. It wasn't quite the answer to my prayer to be a 'back-up' host but at least I would get to feel what it was like to work in a studio and have one more thing to take my mind off my issues. I went in the next week and co-hosted the show with him. It was fun and came very naturally to me. A month later Kofi asked me to step in for him for one show. And that was it. He never came back to the studio! That was six years ago. Albert, the producer is always tickled to bits when he recounts this story.

But I digress.

Six days after I had made this last ditch prayer, I received a phone call from Ernst and Young (EY). It was a Wednesday afternoon and I remember it so vividly.

"Hello, may I speak to Akua Ofori-Boateng?" It was a lady.

"Yes, this is her, who am I speaking with please?"

"Oh hi Akua, my name is Jayne, and I'm calling from Ernst and Young. We came across your CV and think you will be a good candidate for a General Manager role with Bulk. The role reports directly to the MD."

She proceeded to tell me about how they had shortlisted me for an interview to be held in four days' time on the Monday. She apologized for the short notice and asked if she could have my email to send me the job description.

I was so panicked that I didn't ask any questions. I didn't even ask what kind of company Bulk was. I simply gave her my email address and got off the phone as quickly as possible. The whole thing was so surreal that I stared at my email box only half believing that any email would show up from EY. But then a few minutes later, it popped up. There it was, an email from EY asking me to interview for a job with Bulk Inc. the next Monday.

If you ask Me anything in My name, I will do it. John 14:14 (NIV)

That evening, I discovered that Bulk was a state-owned oil and gas company. To be called into interview for that high level a job in an oil and gas company was huge. But in my case it felt miraculous because I don't recall actually applying for the job. This was at a time when everyone wanted to get into the oil and gas industry. It seemed like an incredible opportunity handed to me by God. But then again there was a catch. If this indeed was

God's answer, then it meant the call to priesthood was real.

The fact that this company was state-owned with the MD being a political appointee made by the President of the nation himself, caused me to pause and reflect. I had no doubt that the job was real but I really struggled to believe that they were willing to hand over such a sensitive role to someone who was literally off the streets. This feeling was actually a great source of comfort, because I used it to convince myself that God had goofed and lined me up with a job that I would never get.

Nonetheless, here I was with this one interview opportunity. So I decided to use it to practice my interview skills. I prepared properly for the interview and on that Monday afternoon at about 1:30 p.m., I walked into the hotel Villa Monticello for my 2:00 p.m. interview.

I had some concerns about the time because that afternoon Germany was playing Portugal in a World Cup match and I didn't want to miss it. I know this sounds incredulous, because one would have thought that with such an important opportunity at stake, the last thing on my mind would be a football match. But I couldn't help myself. All I kept thinking about was how I needed to finish the interview and be back home by four in the afternoon.

Again, Paul certainly was not lying when he said that there is a peace which surpasses all understanding. Here I was, unemployed, dirt broke, unable to take care of my child, living off my pensioner mother, unable to make any kind of business work for me. And yet in the face of the one opportunity that could potentially turn my life around, I was concerned about missing a football match. That is God!

> **Rejoice in the Lord always. I will say it again: Rejoice!**
> **Let your gentleness be evident to all. The Lord is**
> **near. Do not be anxious about anything but in every**
> **situation, by prayer and petition, with thanksgiving,**
> **present your requests to God. And the peace of God,**
> **which transcends all understanding, will guard your**
> **hearts and your minds in Christ Jesus. Philippians**
> **4:4-7 (NIV)**

The interview started late. An hour late. Which made the likelihood of me catching my match even smaller. Since the interview was in a hotel and we were all required to wait in the general lobby, it made it impossible to determine who else was there for this particular interview. But as I said, I was so sure that I wouldn't get the job, that it really didn't matter.

Eventually, I was called up. I opened the door to a small conference room with a rather large conference table. Sitting around this table were six men, none of whom I knew. I was asked to sit, which I did. Immediately afterwards, one of the gentlemen piped up with, "Why aren't you a lawyer?" I knew at once that he knew either one or both of my parents. I later discovered that he was the board chairman. I responded by saying, "I see you know my parents." That hung in the air for a few seconds and then the interview proper began.

I don't remember much of it except that I recall being asked what I would do if I was restructuring a company and some people refused to get on board. I answered by saying, "Even God after a while decided that the best way to get the Israelites across from Egypt to Canaan was to just wait till most of them had died off and then move the new generation into the promised land." In other words, at some point we would just have to terminate people.

I answered most of my questions by drawing inferences from Scripture. That surprised me because I didn't realize how much seminary had influenced me. As the interview progressed, I felt like I was standing outside of myself listening to me speak. Just like in church. It was fascinating. I actually sounded really sensible and Christian. Who would have thought!?

Then it ended. I said goodbye politely and rushed off to watch Germany play Portugal in the World Cup.

I was sitting in my mother's room, feet up, snacking on some fruit when my daughter burst in with my phone. By the time she handed it to me, it had just stopped ringing. I didn't recognize the number so I decided to call back after the match. My mother who was watching the game with me said, "Maybe its Bulk calling about your interview." Immediately, I felt the Holy Spirit confirm that she was right. *How could this be?* I thought to myself. *I just finished the interview two hours ago.*

I stared at the phone for a few moments, drew a deep breath and called back. The phone rang. I hated that the phone rang instead of being busy. I walked out of my mother's room, through the sitting room and onto the veranda. I didn't want anyone to hear this call even though technically I didn't know who I was calling. Then he picked up.

"Hello, this is Jacob." I recognized his voice immediately as the MD of Bulk.

Could it really be?

"Hello Jacob, this is Akua, I'm sorry I missed your call."

"Thank you for calling me back. We think you interviewed well and so we are offering you the job." Silence!

"Hello Akua?"

"Oh! Cool! Thank you!" was all I could manage. *Really? Was that the best you could do?* I scolded myself.

"You don't sound happy. Are you sure this is Akua?"

"Yes, yes, yes. it's me. I'm happy." I lifted up my voice a bit trying to sound excited despite the revolution that was unfolding in my life.

"Ok. Well you don't sound like the lady we interviewed. Anyway come in tomorrow and let's talk salary."

"Yes sure, I'll be there. No, it's me and I'm excited. The only thing that can make this better is if Ghana wins the match tonight."

"Oh yes that...I'm not a fan of the Black Stars. They always disappoint."

He was right. They did disappoint.

They lost their World Cup match against the USA that night. But that was the least of my problems. I had just lost a bet to God and I was staring priesthood in the face. I had the weirdest mix of joy and fear that night. I had so many questions. How could God do this to me? How could He seriously ask me to be a priest? How was I going to explain this to anyone? To my mother, to my friends. How does one even start that conversation, "Oh yeah... soooo I've been thinking I want to be a priest now." If anyone said that to me, I would laugh and accuse them of having all kinds of ulterior motives for going into priesthood.

The problem I had though, was that this fulfilment of God's promise was so significant that I couldn't renege on my end of it. The knowledge that I actually had to become a priest weighed so heavily on me that it made me weep. That night I called Reverend Idan. "I told you! I'm a prophet!" He screamed over the phone. He had continued to be a tremendous support and was one of the few people I knew I could talk to about this 'priesthood calling' and not feel like I was being judged. He had always encouraged me to go into priesthood but I just couldn't fathom it. Needless to say, he was giddy with excitement when I told Him what had happened.

I was so dumbfounded and in all honesty frightened. I told my mother that I'd been offered the job and then I went to bed. I said a very short 'thank You' prayer to God. I was so alarmed by this decisive action from God that I decided to minimize my communication with Him, lest He did something else.

I spent weeks pondering over how I was obliged to respond to God's call. Eventually, I told my mother. The day I told her, all my worst fears came to bear. She said, "So because everything in your life has failed, you want to become a priest?" I wanted to tell her then that I didn't actually want to be a priest but I just had to become one. But I didn't, because I didn't think it would make sense to her. Her reaction caused me a great deal of pain. If there were two beings, I wanted to please the most in this world, it was God and my mother. And now here I was making a life decision that pleased one and displeased the other.

Although my mother had been very supportive of my decision to go to seminary, never had it crossed her mind that I would actually apply for the priesthood. Within the Anglican setting, getting a theological degree from a seminary does not make you a priest. Admittedly, most Anglican priests waited until they had been approved as candidates for priesthood before they went to seminary. That notwithstanding, nothing precludes anyone from getting a theological degree if as I had indicated several times they "want to know God better but don't want to become priests." She was blindsided by my decision to apply for the priesthood. But then again so was I. I felt blindsided by God. This was never the plan and yet here we were.

My mother believed that I was giving up on life which is why I was 'on my own' choosing the path for priesthood and that upset her deeply. She was convinced that I was naïve and could not fully appreciate the challenges of priesthood. Over the next few months, she went back and forth between anger where she accused me of foolishness and love where she tried to protect me from making another mistake. She tried to talk me into believing that I was just enamored with the idea of priesthood and was too young and immature to know what I was saying.

Our relationship began to deteriorate and living under her roof became more and more unbearable. Every time my daughter did or said the wrong thing, it somehow was attributed to the fact that I was too engrossed with becoming a priest to pay attention to my daughter. I stopped writing my sermons at home because it felt as if I was disobeying her by writing them under her own roof. One morning, I walked past her while I was getting ready for work and she didn't hear me say good morning. This resulted in a dressing down about how my preaching had gotten to my head and how I now felt too big to even be polite. As a well brought up African child, I knew better than to argue, so I sucked it up and apologized.

I became so distressed by the state of our relationship, that I reported the matter to both Margaret and Canon Lamptey. Margaret was extremely supportive and told me to follow my calling and not look back. She later spoke to my mother, as did Canon Lamptey but all they succeeded in doing was changing her argument from one of 'no' to one of 'not now.' 'Not now' because she believed I should remarry before I become a priest. 'Not now' because in her view, once I became a priest, no man would ever be interested in me. 'Not now' because she believed I should wait till I'm at least fifty years old, because by then, life would have granted me enough wisdom to be able to counsel those who would come to me as a priest.

> "Peter took him aside and began to rebuke him. "Never, Lord!" he said. "This shall never happen to you!"" Jesus turned and said to Peter, "Get behind me, Satan! You are a stumbling block to me; you do not have in mind the concerns of God but merely human concerns." Matthew 16:22-23 (NIV)

In those days I felt like I was between the proverbial rock of God and the hard place of my mother. But after all I had been through, I concluded that my mother was a lot easier to deal with, primarily because I could get away from her whenever I wanted to. All I had to do was leave home early and come back late. But God's pressure was always on, no matter where I went. So again God won. I chose my rock, but I had yet another favor to ask Him.

I had a real chat with God about the job and about our deal. I explained to Him that I was still going to hold up my end of the bargain but I needed some time. The Bulk job was in the bag but I didn't want to have too many drastic changes going on in my life at the same time. So I asked God for a year's grace. I promised Him that the following June, I would apply for priesthood and almost immediately, I felt released to tackle Bulk fully. Maybe because finally, I had fully heeded to God's call.

CHAPTER EIGHT

BULK

God himself has prepared us for this and as a guarantee he has given us his Holy Spirit.
2 Corinthians 5:5 (NIV)

THROWN INTO THE DEEP

The day after the interview, I went to Bulk. I admired and liked Jacob immediately. Although he was on the interview panel, I did not get a chance to truly interact with him. But sitting with him one-on-one, I found him very impressive. He was well spoken, well dressed, intelligent and very confident. His office was nicely set up. Simple but classy. I was struck by the fact that his office door had an electronic lock and needed to be released either by a finger print or with a button underneath his desk. I thought that was very cool. Later, I discovered that practically every important government office in Ghana has a similar door configuration. Who knew?

When I walked in, he was on the phone, sitting behind his desk. He smiled warmly and beckoned me to sit in a small sitting area a few feet from his desk. I sat, and after a few minutes he wrapped up his phone call and joined me. He offered me tea and when I poured my milk before I poured the tea he said, "That's very proper." I smiled. We proceeded to have a very hearty conversation about our lives and our families. He introduced me to his consultant and advisor Judah, and said the three of us were essentially going to be the salvation of Bulk. Judah was an engineer like me and had a world of oil and gas experience. He welcomed me warmly, commented on how impressed he was with my CV and how much he looked forward to working with me. I felt like I was part of an amazing team that was going to change the world, one Bulk at a time. That's how naïve I was.

Jacob told me about a three-day retreat that was about to happen and even though I wasn't due to start for a few more weeks, he wanted to use it as an opportunity to introduce me to the company. He then told me about the factions within the company and the alliances from political and ethnic perspectives. It was all very strange for me. Up until then, I had worked at Proctor & Gamble and at Cummins and neither of them had this level of 'beyond corporate' politics, so I simply couldn't relate. It would only be a matter of time before I would be fully immersed in the politics of Bulk and of Ghana in general.

At the retreat, Jacob led the company to create a two-year strategic plan. It was amazing to watch how drawn the staff were to his charisma. He had everyone eating out of the palm of his hand. I had no idea what the company's atmosphere had been before but it was clear that Jacob was a breath of fresh-air. I fed off that freshness and energy and excitement. And as the General Manager (GM) in charge of Human Resources (HR), Information Technology (IT), Health, Safety, Security and Environment (HSSE), Procurement, and Facilities and Fleet, I was eager to make my mark. My primary role was to spend the next year restructuring the company and I was enthusiastic about how everything was lined up for me to have a truly remarkable time at Bulk. I couldn't have been more wrong.

I showed up for my job that first day and reality hit me like a thunderbolt.

"Why is the internet not working?" Jacob bellowed over the phone at me.

I was eager to please him, so I rushed up to the third floor of the old building trying to figure out where the IT department was. Since there was no orientation process, I had no idea where anything was. Eventually I found the interim IT Manager sitting at his desk. He was a large pleasant man, with a very small desk. I think it was his size that made his desk seem small. He sat in this small room which he shared with two of his subordinates. This was the entire IT department. I took in a deep breath and started with "Good morning."

"Good morning" all three chimed back.

"Why is the internet not working?" I asked, trying to stay calm.

"Oh Madam…it is. It's just that we need to put a router down in the MD's area for it to work there." He said with a bit of a stammer.

"Do we not have a router?" I asked.

"Oh yes Madam, we do."

"So why isn't it installed there?"

"Oh Madam, it can be. Would you like me to install one there?" I was scandalized by his question.

"Errmmm yeah!" I exclaimed sounding irritated.

With that, he scurried off downstairs to install the router. Within thirty minutes, there was internet access for the MD and his secretariat. I returned to my makeshift office trying to figure out what had just happened. Did the IT Manager forget to install the router? He was clearly aware of the problem with Jacob's internet and knew how to solve it. So I couldn't understand why he hadn't just solved it earlier. I couldn't ponder over that for very long because I had more pressing issues, like the fact that I didn't actually have an office.

Probably more pressing was the fact that Jacob had deposited over five hundred confidential documents in my care, all of which needed my attention in terms of approval or denial. Some of the documents were as trivial as buying pencils for the stock room and others were as crucial as paying the overdue electricity bill. They were not in any particular order of importance but regardless of their gravity, I needed an office with a desk and a chair to work on them.

Judah was out of town that first week of work so I took over his office and started to work on the papers. I didn't know where to start from but I figured they were stacked in the order in which they arrived, so I started at the bottom. It wasn't until the Electricity Corporation of Ghana (ECG) cut the power supply to Bulk, and the catering company refused to feed the depot workers, that I realized how critical it was that I went through the pile, in some kind of order, other than the date of arrival.

My borrowed office was however not fit for my purpose. I still needed to find a place that would make my operations more effective. An office that would allow me to handle confidential information and to lock the door when the need arose, even if not with an electronic lock like my MD's door. The Bulk head office was housed in what was originally a three-storey apartment building that had four apartments on each floor. Even if each family had four people, that would mean the building could comfortably hold forty-eight people. Now it was housing over one hundred employees. These employees were scattered all over the building with undersized desks and chairs, in every corner including the hallways and the kitchen. Apart from it being uncomfortable, it was a safety hazard. This should have been the job of the HSSE Manager, except we didn't have one. In fact, part of my job was to create an HSSE department.

But I still needed an office. So I went about trying to organize one. I walked around looking for the Facilities Manager's office and eventually identified a young man who after recognizing me as the GM, literally begged me to allow him to go and fetch the Facilities Manager. I agreed and went back to my temporary desk in Judah's office and waited.

About an hour later, I gave up on my Facilities Manager ever showing up at my office and decided I would go and find him myself. Just as the thought went through my mind, a panting, sweaty, extraordinarily large man walked in. He was over six feet tall and weighed not less than three hundred pounds. He motioned towards the chair across from my desk, clearly asking to sit but was too out of breath to say so. I nodded rapidly and just watched helplessly as he tried to catch his breath. After a few minutes he said, "Madam, I was told you were looking for me." *I was...?* I began to wonder, when it hit me that he was Samson, the Facilities Manager, "Yes, yes. I was looking for your office but the young man said he'd ask you to come." He nodded, still struggling to catch his breath. As I watched Him, I prayed to God, *Dear God, if you keep him alive, I promise I'll never ask him to come up the stairs to my office again.* He lived! God was faithful!

Samson, agreed to get me an office and that was the last time he did anything for me. From then on, he just agreed to everything I asked him to do and then proceeded to do absolutely nothing about it. He wouldn't even attend staff meetings. I guess while I was praying, he must have vowed that if he lived, he'd never do anything for me again. But I had too many fires to fight at the time, so I put him and his department on ice until later that year.

In my first few months of my being at Bulk, everything was so chaotic. I did not even have an appointment letter because the HR Manager had been "out sick" since the day I started. So in addition to all the fires I was fighting, I had to try to get a letter officially hiring me, with a salary and benefits, so I could get paid and end my poverty!

By the end of that first three months, I had been so busy fighting all these challenges that my main job of restructuring the company had fallen off my radar. In those early days, I felt so helpless and overwhelmed. I had never worked in an organization that was so completely dysfunctional. Nothing worked! Everything was about party politics. Where party politics didn't prevail, then it came down to ethnicity. Patriotism was not even on the table as motivation for people to work. Everyone was in it for themselves and no one else.

What was fascinating was how at 4:00 p.m., the various cliques in the company would start gathering as if they were about to have a conference. Then between 4:30 p.m. and 5:00 p.m. they would all start leaving the office in droves. Clique after clique would exit the building and by 5:00 p.m., the last soul would leave. It was like watching the exodus of God's people every day.

One afternoon, Jacob asked me how the restructuring was going. He met me on the stairwell and asked, "How come my company is not restructured?" That night, I went down on my knees and I told God all my problems and I asked Him nicely to help me out.

If you believe, you will receive whatever you ask for in prayer. Matthew 21:22 (NIV)

IF GOD BE FOR US, WHO CAN BE AGAINST US?

From then on, I felt like Bulk was mine to conquer. I went into work the next day and called a general staff meeting with all fifty-two people in my team. That morning, I informed them that things were going to change. I implemented what I called "standing meetings" where all of us would meet and stand in a common area for not more than thirty minutes every Monday morning at nine. In that meeting, each manager had five minutes to present to the entire department, what they had done the week before and their plans for the new week. As part of that meeting, I implemented a one Ghana Cedi penalty for each minute a person was late. I also put a low ranking officer in charge of monitoring late comers and collecting the fees. The next week, I was deliberately late by five minutes and I showed up with my five cedis cash in hand. Now there was no excuse for any one not to pay up. Those meetings were the beginning of the turnaround at Bulk for myself and my team.

Through those meetings, I discovered that a lot of the workers of Bulk were actually very hard working and were full of brilliant ideas that just needed to be channeled. After a few months, our thirty minute meetings started getting longer because each department was accomplishing so much more that it just took longer to report on it all. I encouraged the Managers of the various departments to allow their subordinates to present on behalf of their teams. That resulted in a lot of laughter as junior officers made mistakes and got lightly scolded by their respective Managers. It was great fun. And we seemed to be always laughing. I would later discover that the laughter and joy that emerged from our department was a great source of irritation and envy to other people who eventually made it their mission to 'get me'.

In the first few months, we made enough money from late fees to throw a party for ourselves. That, however, only happened once because people got tired of paying the money so they just showed up on time. Everyone was on board and worked very hard. Everyone except Samson. He never showed up. Not once. His team came but not him. I was so frustrated with his insubordination and general disrespect for myself and my team that one night I went down on my knees and I prayed saying, "Dear God, Samson is a thorn in my side. Please remove him from my team. Amen."

By my sixth month, the restructuring was in full swing. God had stopped reminding me about priesthood. I was still preaching in church and I was making decent money so my family had gained a brand new respect for me. More importantly, the issue of how I was going to get the money required for my daughter's school fees had been resolved. Generally, things were looking up. It was a clear testament of God's goodness. To think that just a few months earlier, I was in dire financial straits. And now, here I was having taken on the task of restructuring a very essential state owned company. For me it was proof that God can indeed make a way where there appears to be no way.

> **Forget the former things; do not dwell on the past. See, I am doing a new thing! Now it springs up; do you not perceive it? I am making a way in the wilderness and streams in the wasteland. Isaiah 43:18-19 (NIV)**

Bulk afforded me the opportunity to see parts of Ghana, I'd never imagined I would ever visit. I spent months travelling to the various Bulk locations across the country to talk about the restructuring and to get the views of the staff on how the company needed to change. I had chosen a bottom-up approach where every single employee had an opportunity to contribute. Jacob with his magnetic personality, was extraordinarily supportive and the entire company bought into the vision and followed his lead. It was an incredibly exhilarating time for me to be part of the transformation of this enterprise and it felt like God was finally shinning some light on me because I had agreed to become a priest.

Within a year of my employment, we were ready to push the go button on this restructuring. Together, as a company, we had developed a new organizational structure and now needed to transition into our new roles. Several employees had expressed an interest to apply for jobs in other parts of the company and since there was no real way of selecting who should get which job, we agreed that we would put all the jobs up for people to apply as they wished. At least I thought that was the agreement.

To make sure no one had an unfair advantage, we decided that all job applications would be electronic and all employees would receive the list of openings at the same time in their email. This required the IT department to put in some extra work. In preparation for this, I called a meeting with the IT Manager to discuss how we could send out companywide messages to make sure that all staff received the same information at the same time.

In the middle of this meeting, my door flew open and one of my Managers, Gabriella, burst into my office yelling frantically about how Samson had fallen down. Immediately, the image of his gargantuan figure having fallen down the stairs popped up in my head and I wondered why he was climbing the stairs in the first place.

I tried to get some details but she just kept yelling, "He's fallen down! He's fallen down!" The IT Manager and I rushed out after her and all three of us raced down the stairs to the reception area. There was a lot of frantic movements in the lobby with several employees rushing out to sit in their cars. My eyes met the receptionist's eyes. She was frozen with fear, with her mouth open and her eyes wide. Without asking her anything, she volunteered, "They've taken him to Nyaho!"

Now, I understood the rush to the car park and I also rushed towards my car and jumped in. With the IT Manager in my passenger seat, we took off towards Nyaho Medical Centre. As I was rushing out of the Bulk lobby, a gentleman who looked vaguely familiar said to me, "Madam, I'll follow in my car." I couldn't figure out who he was or why he was following me but I didn't have time to ask.

I brought my car to a screeching halt at the Nyaho car park and rushed towards the hospital's emergency door. As I walked briskly through the parking lot towards the group of Bulk staff standing around the entrance of the hospital, I noticed that they were talking to a doctor outside the hospital and were hovering around the SUV that had transported Samson to the hospital. One Facilities and Fleet officer, James, walked towards me with tears streaming down his face, "He's gone!" he said with his voice quivering. "He's gone!"

"What!? He's gone!?"

I took his hand and walked even more briskly towards the SUV. And there, lying in the back of the vehicle was Samson. Dead. I was stunned.

I was suddenly flooded with fear and guilt. Could this be God's answer to my prayer? No way! God would never do that, I asked Him to remove him from my team, not kill him! This would not be the first time God appeared to have misunderstood my prayer but this time it was scary. As I stood there pondering all these things, I heard the doctor say that he would not accept the body because he was dead on arrival and had not died in his care. Then he said, "I need someone to sign for the fact that you brought him here dead." Suddenly, the crowd started to disperse. Nobody wanted to sign. It was like watching fleas leave a dead dog. They all just walked backwards and turned their backs on Samson. Then someone said, "Our MD has travelled and our GM is the most senior person here." I had no choice, I signed. I felt like I was accepting responsibility for his death. Then the doctor said, "OK, now you have to take the body away."

I didn't know what to do. So I called the on-again-off-again HR Manager, who just became hysterical on the phone, wailing and crying. I was so frustrated with her total loss of control that I told her I'd call her back and I hung up. Suddenly, I found myself alone in the car park with Nathaniel my IT Manager, the driver of the SUV, James, the officer who broke the news of the death to me and the lifeless body of Samson. None of us knew what to do. I didn't even know where to find a morgue. Then out of the blue, I heard a man say behind me, "Madam, do you need help getting him into a morgue?" I spun around and there stood the familiar looking man from the lobby who said he would follow me. "Yes! Please, can you help us?"

Apparently this man was ex-military and was good friends with the head of the 37 Military Hospital morgue director. He had been in the lobby waiting to meet me to discuss a project he was interested in. That was why he looked familiar, we had met before and I had agreed to meet him that afternoon. And right there in front of us, he made one phone call, hung up and said, "He said we should bring the body but we must hurry because they are about to close." A wave of relief washed over me. I felt it was God telling me, "I've got you." We all loaded up into our various cars and rushed off to the 37 military hospital to deposit the body.

> **But if I were you, I would appeal to God; I would lay my cause before him. He performs wonders that cannot be fathomed, miracles that cannot be counted. Job 5:8-9 (NIV)**

The next thing was how to break the news to his wife. In my naivety, I had just assumed we would go over to her home and tell her. But apparently that is a big no-no in Ghanaian culture. And so what I thought would be a thirty-minute affair became a long drawn out four-hour matter. By the time I got home from the morgue and telling his wife and kids that their husband and daddy wasn't coming home, it was almost midnight. I took a long hot shower and I prayed. I prayed for Samson and his family, especially his children and then I asked God 'Why?'

He was silent.

I lay in bed for hours just staring at the ceiling. Had I done something wrong? Was it bad that I prayed asking God to get Samson to be taken off my team? It had to be a coincidence! There was no way God could be so extreme. This was not what I wanted. Not death. Oh my goodness! That night I cried myself to sleep.

> **A person's days are determined; you have decreed the number of his months and have set limits he cannot exceed. Job 14:5 (NIV)**

A VALUABLE LESSON IN HUMAN BEHAVIOUR

The office was naturally subdued the next day. Several people were, of course, hearing the news for the first time. Most people grouped in their cliques of old and had caucus meetings. I decided to let the restructuring go-date lapse for the week, to allow people to mourn and tell and retell the story of his passing. It eventually came to light that he had suffered a massive heart attack whilst talking to one of his staff in his office. It appears he died before he even hit the ground. I thanked God for his life and tried to focus on my work. I called Nathaniel back into my office for us to continue the meeting we were having the previous day before we both had to rush out on the basis of Samson's situation. We agreed that in the face of what had happened, we would let the week run out and send the messages over the next weekend on the Sunday night.

That Sunday, Nathaniel and I stayed in the office till about 2:00 AM, setting up systems so that on Monday morning, the whole company would be greeted with the launch of the restructuring program. A part of which was the opportunity to contest for any job of their choosing up to three jobs. Jacob was fully informed and in agreement. The restructuring team was aware. So we hit the go button and we went to bed.

At 7:00 a.m. on Monday morning, I received my first protest call. It was the leader of the Senior Staff Union, Pierre. He was a leading figure on the restructuring team and had been extraordinarily helpful and influential. Somehow, he had assumed that he would be exempted from putting in a bid for a job. In fact, he had expressed to me which job he wanted and assumed I would just give it to him for good behavior. That is where he had it all wrong. No one was exempted, from justifying why they should be handed the job they wanted. Not even me.

"Akua, this is not good. This is not what we discussed." I reminded him that we had discussed it and he had been on the road with me promoting it but had somehow seen himself as exempt. The conversation did not end well. It was the first of many hostile conversations that would transpire between us. Until eventually, we stopped speaking to each other altogether.

Next came a call from the leader of the Junior Staff Union, Thomas, "Madam this is brilliant. Now we can have justice in this company. Those who think they are good should prove it. I had doubted Jacob before, but now I am convinced!"

Then Jacob called from the UK, "Good job. Keep a low profile today and don't answer any questions. I'll be back this afternoon."

At 11:00 a. m., the big guns came out.

"Akua, I understand the staff are very upset and demonstrating by wearing red bands on their hands." This was the Board Chairman.

"No sir, there is no protest. The red bands are to signify that we are mourning Samson. Even I have one on."

"Oh ok. So there is no problem?" he asked very calmly.

"No sir."

"Ok good. If there is any problem, call me. You're doing a good job."

I felt really good. However, just as I started to relax, another board member called, "Akua, what the hell are you doing? How could you do this without informing the board? You need to reverse this immediately!"

I could just feel myself losing my temper. I hated being bullied and this was precisely what he was trying to do.

"Sir, with all due respect, I don't work for or report to the board. I have full approval from the MD and until he tells me to reverse this, we will continue as planned." I was amazed at how calm I sounded. Inside, I was far from calm. My heart was racing in me and felt like it needed more room than my chest cavity could provide.

"The board is unaware and I have received several phone calls complaining about you in particular. In fact, I'm coming over now." With that, he hung up and I imagine stormed out of wherever he was and into his car.

I tried not to panic. I prayed and asked God for boldness. I couldn't call Jacob because I knew he was somewhere in the middle of his six-hour flight from London. I called Nathaniel into my office. We talked for about an hour and he somehow managed to make me laugh. It calmed me down but not totally. I kept waiting for Mr. Arthur, the angry board member, to barge in and hand my backside to me.

While Nathaniel and I were still chatting, my Personal Assistant walked in and informed me that an emergency board meeting was in session and that I had been summoned.

"In session!?" I exclaimed.

"Yes Madam! In session. All the General Managers and Managers have been informed that the board would like to see them but the board wants to see you first." I looked at Nathaniel incredulously.

"Did you know about this?"

"No-ooo!" He could barely get the word out.

"How were the General Managers informed?" I asked my PA.

"By email Madam."

I looked at Nathaniel and he shrugged helplessly.

"Get to the bottom of this." I said to him under my breath.

"Ok." I said to my PA, "Tell the board, I'm coming."

The walk from my office to the boardroom was like walking the plank. All the staff were out and whispering in their various cliques and caucus groups and as I approached, they would quiet down. I made a point of smiling and nodding at everyone whose eye I could catch and I put an extra spring in my step.

Inside me though, I was comatose. When I opened the door to the boardroom, there they were, the full board save the board chairman and the MD.

> **Let your compassion quickly meet our needs because we are on the brink of despair. Psalm 79:8 (NLT)**

"Sit down Akua" Mr. Arthur instructed.

I sat next to a board member I liked. He was a doctor and had always been very nice to me. Mr. Arthur was being very diplomatic and asked me to explain what had happened. It was as if he expected that in my explanation I would somehow implicate myself. It appeared from where he sat that my crime was not informing the board. And from where I sat, I believed that this was an operational issue and it was the job of the MD to inform the board and not mine. In fact, I didn't even think the board had any right to give me instructions or even speak to me in the absence of my MD.

I sat, and a hard interrogation began.

I teared up several times during the meeting but I was determined not to cry in front of them. I say interrogation, because that is what it was. An interrogation and a sentencing all at once. But I stood my ground. I refused to reverse what I had done without a direct instruction from my MD. The second phase of the interrogation was what I call the betrayal. The board called in the other Managers and General Managers.

These individuals, some of whom had actually sent me emails lobbying me for jobs as part of the restructuring, walked in and one by one denied all knowledge of the restructuring exercise. They denied their involvement in the roadshows we had done, denied the various retreats we had been on and denied the weekly meetings with the HR consultants to clearly define their departments. They denied everything and just plain lied, saying that Jacob and I were single handedly restructuring the company.

I was shocked!

The only Manager who didn't lie that day was Nathaniel. He had not been invited to the meeting. I would later find out that the whole 'emergency board meeting' was a set up where the Board Secretary had sent out emails to every General Manager and Manager informing them about the meeting and he deliberately excluded Nathaniel and me. It was essentially a coup d'etat and I was furious. As I listened to each Manager, tell their made up stories, I sent Jacob a WhatsApp message saying, "If you don't come to the office in the next thirty minutes, you'll have no office to come to!" His response was, "getting my bags."

> **Be strong and courageous, do not be afraid or tremble at them, for the LORD your God is the one who goes with you, He will not fail you or forsake you. Deuteronomy 31:6 (NIV)**

When Jacob walked into the meeting, Mr. Arthur stood up and said very dismissively, "Oh Jacob you are here. We were just having a little chat with Akua." He downplayed the whole affair and Jacob being the master politician he is, played right along. I must admit I was in awe of both of them. When Mr. Arthur left, it dawned on me how truly controlled and masterful a person Jacob is and as large as he loomed in my eyes, he only increased further. I placed him on an even higher pedestal and observed him more closely, wanting to learn everything I could from him.

From that day forward, my eyes were opened to a completely new dimension of human nature. I realized that people can be extremely self-serving, to the point where they would not blink before betraying another, as long as the betrayal serves their parochial interest. Apart from God, we can expect no one to come through for us.

With the coup attempt thwarted, I put in a formal petition that the Board Secretary be sacked for a breach of board protocol. Jacob and the Board Chairman called me in and assured me that the necessary sanctions would be meted out. In the end, he received what in my view was a reward. He was scolded by the MD and the Board Chairman and reassigned to "Siberia." Siberia, essentially, is a paid vacation where you are assigned to a nameless, do-nothing job, in which you still get paid at the same level you were at before.

I guess the punishment, if you want to call it that, is that you have to show up at work as you normally would and just do nothing. For a government institution, that was about as much punishment as he was ever going to get. But my battle was far from over. Those opposed to the restructuring methodology, namely Mr. Arthur and Pierre, ramped up their game and the flames I was walking through raged on.

This is what the Lord says to you: 'Do not be afraid or discouraged because of this vast army. For the battle is not yours but God's. 2 Chronicles 20:15. (NIV)

CHAPTER NINE

WHY? WERE YOU NOT INFORMED?

**When you pass through the waters, I will be with you;
and when you pass through the rivers, they will not
sweep over you. When you walk through the fire, you
will not be burned; the flames will not set you ablaze.
Isaiah 43:2 (NIV)**

Pierre, in his frustration, took the matter to the media and decried Jacob. That was when the true roller coaster ride began. By seven O'clock in the morning, as I was taking my daughter to school, the airwaves were full of how Bulk was on 'fire' because all the employees had been summarily dismissed and asked to "re-apply" for their jobs. I couldn't believe the extent of the media dishonesty and not being a politician, or a public figure of any sort, I was completely out of my depth. The media was a thing I avoided like the plague and I just didn't know what to do.

I called Jacob and he was as cool as cucumber. He said to me, "Just remain calm, walk slowly and make sure you smile at everyone today." Jacob seemed to thrive on chaos and I admired that quality in him. I needed structure and order to thrive. That level of chaos made me very unsure of myself. I prayed all the way to the office that morning. I prayed every prayer I knew and tried to find Scriptures that would encourage me but by the time I got to the office, I had found no boldness. Instead, I was nauseous with fear.

As the good Lord would have it, I stepped out of my car and walked directly into a brand new fire, which took my mind off the one that was already raging. The security company we used was facing a boycott by their staff for poor working conditions and the result was that none of them showed up to guard any of the facilities assigned to them. On a normal day, this would have been a great source of irritation but on that day, it was a very welcome distraction.

At about mid-morning, while I was dealing with this and avoiding all media, Jacob called and said, "I want you to prepare a termination letter for Pierre." I wasn't particularly surprised because it was a direct breach of contract for a member of staff to speak to the media about anything happening in the company without explicit permission from the MD. As calm as he was, I could tell Jacob was seething.

Now I was focused. I needed to identify all the labor laws and employee conditions that Pierre had breached in order to terminate him. I also needed to figure out how to get the security crew back on our premises. I decided to tackle the termination issue first. I called-in the deputy HR Manager, since the HR Manager was still recovering from the death of Samson and as such, was on some kind of continuation of her leave. The deputy HR Manager was called Judith. I liked her because she was goal driven. She was one of those people who, if you gave a task, you could go to sleep. I spoke with her in confidence about the Pierre assignment and she was all over it.

She liked Pierre and was actually quite good friends with him but she agreed that his blatant breach of company policy was a terminable offence. "After all," she said, "rules are rules." Then she collected everything I needed to justify the termination.

I spent the next hour drafting what in my opinion was the perfect termination letter. It was like a poem, a thing of beauty and I relished writing it. I wished I was signing it, just to put that final bullet in Pierre's head. But alas, I was only a GM and not the MD. I printed the letter on the best quality paper we had in the office. The type we used for really important letters. The regular stuff would not do. Not for Pierre. This termination was special. I took it over to Jacob's office, he read it and asked me to leave it with him.

If it were now, I would have handled that whole situation very differently. I have come to understand that what people dish out to us, be it kindness or spitefulness, is really just their cry for help. It is an overflow of what is actually going on inside them and as Christians, we have a responsibility to reach out to them in love and compassion. Pierre was really just crying out for help with all his antics. What he needed was validation and assurance of his inclusion. I was however quite immature myself and so I executed my 'duty' unflinchingly, without compassion for my fellow person.

> **Be kind to one another, tenderhearted, forgiving one another, as God in Christ forgave you. Ephesians 4:32 (NIV)**

Meanwhile, my HSSE Manager, Silas, had successfully communicated to the security company that their contract, which by the way had expired several months earlier, was not going to be renewed, and that we were about to put out a tender for a new security company. That message triggered a lot more activity than I had anticipated. Apparently, the security company belonged to some big and important person in the government and so refusing to renew their contract and finding a new company was just not one of the available options. The board chairman of the security company called and asked for a meeting with me, so I offered to meet with him the next day at 3:00 p.m.

Then it happened! Jacob signed and delivered the letter to Pierre.

The whole office was in a tizzy. I don't think anyone had ever been terminated from Bulk before that day. Certainly not to my knowledge. People just got transferred to other roles or to "Siberia". I was sorry I wasn't there for the actual termination when Jacob handed him the letter. I had wanted to return that beaming smile that he had so generously offered me on the day the board summoned and interrogated me. When I got home, I thanked God. But He was silent. On hindsight, He probably was not pleased with how much joy I derived from Pierre's downfall. Or maybe He just knew what was coming next and wanted me to brace myself.

The next day, I decided to ignore the chatter on Pierre and focus on my security issue. The Board Chairman of the security company had agreed to the meeting time of 3:00 p.m. but for some reason, he didn't want to meet at the Bulk head office. He wanted to meet at the Fiesta Royale Hotel. I found it odd but I obliged.

MORE BETRAYAL

By 2:45 p.m., I was at the hotel. I saw several other Bulk employees there but that wasn't unusual because we often had trainings at the hotel and it was a popular place for lunch and meetings in general. I sat in the lobby with Silas, fine tuning our strategy for the meeting and who would say what. About fifteen minutes later, the Board Chairman of the security company showed up and we began to discuss the matter. As we sat in the lobby talking, I kept seeing more and more Bulk staff walk through the lobby. It sort of registered as odd but I ignored it. Then I saw Mr. Arthur, the board member walk in. Immediately, I excused myself from my security meeting and headed towards him. "Good afternoon sir, what's happening? How come everyone is coming out here?" I asked casually, pretending like we had not just emerged from a verbal war. "Oh we are having a meeting with some of the union staff to discuss the Pierre issue." I knew immediately something wasn't right, but I had no idea how bad it really was. I decided to call Jacob as soon as my security meeting was done.

Just as I was wrapping up my meeting, the Board Chairman of Bulk walked into the lobby. He and I had a fantastic relationship, so I knew with him I would get to the bottom of things and probably not have to talk to Jacob. I stood up from my chair and nodded at him. He made a bee line for me and said rather sternly "I was in the office looking for you."

"Oh, I'm sorry, I was here working out this security issue." I answered honestly.

"Well, where you were needed was in the meeting with the MD planning the press conference."

"Press conference! We are having a press conference?"

"Why? Were you not informed?"

"No sir, this is the first I'm hearing of it. What is it about?"

"Well, Pierre has apologized and Jacob has decided to reinstate him."

I couldn't believe it! How could Jacob do this? Why would he not discuss it with me? I let the Board Chairman know how irritated I was and told him I would not attend the press conference since I was not invited. My ego had stepped in front and center. He said he understood but asked me to come, if not for my job, then for my relationship with him. That made me feel valued, so I obliged. I walked with him to the hotel's large conference center. He went through the front entrance and sat at the podium. I went in through the rear entrance and sat on the seat closest to the door.

The hall was buzzing with activity. And the media was everywhere. Every major media house was there. Since all Bulk PR issues fell directly under my purview, the only way this press conference could be pulled off was through the Communications Manager. And the only way he could do that without my permission was if he had permission directly from the MD with explicit instructions to keep me out of the loop. Incredible! I couldn't understand why Jacob would organize such a large event and opt not to tell me. Yes, I would have disagreed with him strongly but since he was my boss, if he insisted, I would have executed it. Anyway it was done. So I was going to watch it unfold.

Within a few minutes of my arrival, the Communications Manager, climbed the podium and started asking people to sit and quiet down. No surprise there. I knew he had to be involved. The noise level reduced but it was by no means quiet. Suddenly, the hall was filled with flashing lights and the sound of cameras clicking. Jacob walked in like a superstar, followed closely by Thomas, the leader of the Junior Staff Union. He was followed by a few Junior Staff Union executives and then bringing up the rear was Pierre.

I was amazed. I had never imagined that Pierre, after betraying Jacob and after all the insults Jacob had rained down on him for going to the media would now share a high table with him. While I, the faithful servant of Jacob, sat at the back of the room watching events unfold without fore knowledge. At this point, I knew that God was just putting me on ice so I could get past myself. A few speeches were given and then Jacob spoke. I don't remember much of what he said but I do recall him saying, "To err is human and to forgive is divine, and Pierre is only human..." I concluded the sentence under my breath by saying, "...and I guess you are divine." Then to add insult to injury, Pierre got up to speak. As if by divine intervention, in that very instant, I got a phone call that would later have a huge impact on my career.

Since I was sitting right by the door, it was easy to step out, "Hello, this is Akua."

"Akua this is Jürgen. We just got a letter saying we were not successful in the pipeline tender." He was calm but there was something very dark in his voice.

"Yes, that is correct, we determined that your competitor was a better fit for us."

With that, he flew off the handle and ripped into me over the phone about how he felt cheated and believed the system was rigged. I tried to assure him that it wasn't. But given that I was feeling hard-done-by and betrayed at that moment, I don't think I tried very hard to defend Bulk. He wasn't convinced. He threatened to sue me and then hung up.

I went back into the conference hall to listen to the tail end of Pierre's 'victory speech.' I was so dejected that I didn't wait till the end of the press conference. On my way out, I called my brother Kwafo. He was furious and suggested I quit immediately. But Jacob's charisma still had such a hold on me that in as much as I was upset, quitting sounded extreme. So I called my mum. She said, "You need to start finding a way out of Bulk." I believe now that those messages to leave Bulk were the first reminders from God that this job was one part of a two-part deal. And that we were rapidly approaching the one-year mark where I needed to apply for the priesthood.

A PACT WITH GOD IS A PACT WITH GOD

Until then, priesthood had fallen completely to the background. I knew what the agreement with God was, but since He had stopped giving me pressure about it, I had gotten comfortable. I felt very alone all of a sudden, just like I had felt when I was in the USA. I went back to the office brooding and pondering. I worked late and avoided Jacob, even though I knew he was back in the building and was just down the hall from me in his barricaded office. At about 9:00 p.m., I left and went for a long drive. The drive took me to a jazz club called Plus 233. I sat in my car for about an hour and watched people dancing to live jazz. I tried to pray but I was too angry. So I just sat. Then my phone rang. It was Jacob.

"Where are you?" He asked as if he couldn't believe that I was not in a meeting debriefing after such an activity filled day.

"I'm in my car" I answered coldly.

"I need you in my office" he said, as if I owed him work after 5:00 p.m.

"It's 11:00 p.m., whatever it is, we can sort it out tomorrow."

"No, it's a letter the board expects by tomorrow morning justifying the reinstatement of Pierre."

I almost lost it. Did he seriously expect me to come in and essentially reverse the letter I wrote terminating Pierre? That day, I knew God was with me because my answer surprised even me and his response surprised me more. "Jacob, I can't be a part of anything that has to do with Pierre anymore. I'm sorry but I'm not coming in. You're on your own." I believed my termination was up next, or maybe I hoped it was. But all he said was, "I understand, get some rest. I'll see you in the morning." And with that, the Pierre matter died. Sort of.

The next day, Pierre boldly walked into my office to "greet" me. I was very polite but he was cold. He made clear to me that the battle lines had been drawn and I needed to "watch my back." I informed him that I was not a good person to threaten and I asked him to leave my office. After this encounter, the pressure from God to go into the priesthood returned full force.

> **But the Advocate, the Holy Spirit, whom the Father will send in my name, will teach you all things and will remind you of everything I have said to you. John 14:26 (NIV)**

Now, more than ever, I was determined to get the restructuring done. I was fueled by the anger I felt from all the betrayals and heartaches I had been subjected to over the past few days. This was very much the me of old, driven by negativity. Later in life as a priest, this particular time in my life made me see that all of us can be used by God despite the darkness that still lurks in us. Here I was, called by God Himself to be a priest and yet I still struggled with anger and revenge. It taught me that no one is so good that they deserve to be used by God and in the same vein no one is so bad that they cannot be used by God. We each have areas of light and dark in us and God, as He pleases, shines light in those dark places at the right time.

Pierre had grown brand new wings, and horns I might add. He began to agitate and stir up staff against anyone who was an advocate for the restructuring. But he had an Achilles heel. Everyone knew that he had been a huge advocate of the restructuring, at the time he thought a job would be handed to him, so it was difficult for him to push back too hard. Jacob was very calm about all this agitation. He strongly believed that he had decapitated Pierre. I remember he would say, "When you cut off a snake's head, all that is left is rope." One day, I got so fed-up with hearing him make this claim that I breached my own rule to never speak of Pierre again and I said to Jacob, "This snake will grow a new head!" It turned out to be a very prophetic statement.

As part of the restructuring, we determined that we needed an HR consultant to help us navigate the recruitment process as well as the assessment of non-managerial staff strengths, so we could place them in the right roles. I was so concerned about appearing biased in the selection of the employees that I didn't even get involved in the selection for the HR consultant. I left it to the Procurement Manager to do and trusted they would identify the right person for the job.

A few weeks later, the Procurement Manager walked into my office and said, "Madam, we have concluded on the selection of the consultant and the lady we chose says she would like to meet you."

"Sure, let her up" I said, too engrossed in my computer to realize that the person was just a few steps behind him at the door.

"She's here." I looked up and there she was, Sika, my secondary school guidance counsellor. I hadn't seen her in twenty years and she looked exactly the same. Tall, elegant and oozing with confidence. We were so excited to see each other, we hugged and laughed and generally celebrated. I'm not sure when the Procurement Manager left but by the time we settled down he was gone. Sika and I talked for about an hour about everything that had transpired in the last twenty years. How she had left GIS and started up her own consultancy. I, of course, told her about my down-again-up-again life. She suggested that I should come and see her for professional counseling, especially after having gone through a divorce. I smiled politely and immediately dismissed it as unnecessary. But I would find out that I was dismissing the voice of God. When she left, I smiled up at God and told Him I thought He was a jolly good fellow. "Good looking out" I said out loud, not about the counseling, which I had no intention of doing, but about the fact that I already knew the person who had been selected to get me through the restructuring.

Jacob introduced another consultant, who was a specialist in a system which would make Bulk about eighty percent paperless. Between Sika and that gentleman, we got it done. Bulk was restructured. People were in new roles with new salaries, which had not been revised in over ten years. Jacob and all management members could sit and approve requests from anywhere in the world just by pressing a few buttons on their phone. The internet worked, the lunch menu was good and the mood in the company lifted. Jacob was a hero. And God was on me to hold up my end of our deal.

One morning Jacob said, "I want you to move us into a new office building." He was right. In as much as so much was working better in the company, we were still sitting on top of each other. In typical Jacob style, he had already decided which building he wanted us to move into, the lease was signed and so I assumed all I needed to do was sort out the logistics of moving people. I was dead wrong.

The building he had selected for us to move into was lovely on the outside but on the inside, it was a mess. I needed the Facilities and Fleet department to step up like the IT department had stepped up before. As fate would have it, the departure of Samson, meant that I now had a free hand to work with the staff in the department without opposition. With a few of my old faithful, Nathaniel, Judith and Silas, we kicked the project off.

The first thing we needed to do was get the building finished on the inside. The team, led by James, the Facilities and Fleet officer worked with military precision and incredible coordination. It was impressive to come in on a Sunday morning on my way to church to find out that the IT guys had spent Saturday night in the building making sure that the cabling was done right. That was when I completely dispelled the misconception I had that government workers are not dedicated to their companies and to the country at large.

I had promised Jacob that in exactly ninety days we would pull off the feat of relocating the entire company. So we set a date of March 15th for when the first person would move in. After that, if all went according to plan, everyone would be in a new seat within the next seven days. The plan was to move people by department, according to the restructured company and the new roles each person now held. Legal was the smallest department so we chose to move them in first.

The day before the move, the head of the Legal department walked into my office and informed me that my decision to move the company the next day was bound to fail because as she put it, "Not only is the building dirty, there is no running water or electricity." She concluded with, "I can assure you I am not moving into that building in that state." Knowing that I had lined up the cleaners and the water company, I simply told her with all the disdain I could muster to reach back out to me in 24 hours' time.

Now the pressure was on. We had managed to pull everything together, from the internet which would be split between the two sites for a period of two weeks to ensure a seamless move, all the way to ensuring that there would be food in both cafeterias. The only challenge we had was electricity. So the plan was to bring in a massive generator by crane to power the building until we could sort out our issues with the electricity company.

The pressure was truly on. I had 24 hours to get the generator in the office, hooked up and tested before this legal lady came back at me with her victory dance. I called in the part of the team that was responsible for it and they assured me that a crane was on its way to the generator location to fetch it and put in on a truck.

This was at 10 a.m.

At noon I got a call that the crane had toppled.

What!!??

How could they have chosen so small a crane that the weight of the generator toppled it? I couldn't even scream about it because everyone was scrambling so hard to find a solution. So I closed my door, sat at my desk and prayed. I'm not quite sure what I prayed but I remember telling God to just fix it. As I prayed, I remembered Jacob's words from the day of the restructuring issue, "Just remain calm, walk slowly and make sure you smile at everyone today."

So, I did just that, I walked out of my office and went down to the cafeteria, which was full of people having lunch. I spotted an empty chair at the legal lady's table, so I walked over, smiled broadly at everyone on the table. I set my phone on the table to hold the spot and then went over to the buffet counter to get myself some lunch. All the time I was feverish inside, wondering how on earth I was going to explain to the whole company that the relocation had to be delayed.

After lunch, I tried to get some work done. I was determined not to follow up on the generator. Around 4:00 p. m., I called Nathaniel to ask what he was up to. He said he was at the new office working out his IT stuff. I enjoyed his company so I decided to drive over and hang out with him. I drove in, parked and as I walked into the building through the front door, I heard the loud rumble of a turning engine and almost simultaneously a workman shouted in a loud voice, "Switch over!!" I turned to my left where the sound and the voice came from and right there in front of me like a knight in shining armor was this massive Cummins generator, purring as if to say, "I'm home." I could have hugged it.

The workman who shouted was one of my allies called Christian. I rushed over to him to find out how on earth the generator had arrived and had been set up so quickly. His response, "Madam, when they said it was for you, I took over. The devil is a liar." We both laughed and I left him to it. That day, I realized the extent to which God will go to help us. Christian had abandoned whatever he needed to get done for the day just to see me through my situation.

When Moses' hands grew tired, they took a stone and put it under him and he sat on it. Aaron and Hur held his hands up...one on one side, one on the other... so that his hands remained steady till sunset. Exodus 17:12 (NIV)

In the end, the relocation was not too painful. We had a few glitches but we pulled it off. Once we had moved in and settled down, God turned up the heat. I started to feel the burden of priesthood in my heart again and I knew the time had truly come for me to fulfill my promise to God. The restructuring was over. Jacob was in his element. And the company appeared to be doing well. Most employees were well adjusted and earning at rates commensurate with their counterparts in the industry. The company made a profit and you could tell that we were slowly becoming a well-oiled machine. But I was unhappy.

My emptiness of old had returned but this time, I knew it was because it had been a year and I still had not fulfilled my promise to God. Increasingly, I became unhappy with the work at Bulk, despite the progress we had made. It was now an election year and the backbiting, self-interests and acerbic machinations were incessant and quite frankly very uncomfortable for me. Everything seemed to get to me, the heightened political tension and Jacob's constant shifting goalposts based on what was most politically expedient as opposed to what was right for the company. I complained several times but each time he somehow trivialized my concerns and attributed them to my being religious or my being a woman, or both.

When I accepted the role at Bulk, I genuinely believed that I could make a difference. And I believed Jacob when he said he wanted Bulk to stand out as the one State Owned Enterprise (SOE) that all other SOE's could emulate. And I wanted to lend all my training, my skills and talents to being a part of it. I wanted Bulk to be a shining example of the excellence that can happen when public servants truly dedicate themselves to their state. But I realized that unlike me, Jacob was wise enough to know that it would probably never happen. The system was too chocked with personal, political and ethnic interests for there ever to truly be one accord.

I still hold a candle to the idea that one day, all of us as citizens will realize that the work entrusted to us, be it work in the public sector or in the private sector, is work we must do to honor God. And we must honor Him by giving off our best and shun the practice of putting our political, ethnic, or personal interests at the center of everything we do.

> **Whatever you do, work at it with all your heart, as working for the Lord, not for human masters. Colossians 3:23 (NIV)**

One morning, I went to Jacob and I said, "I'm going to go into the Priesthood." He didn't seem at all surprised. In fact, it was almost as though he had been waiting for me to tell him. "That's good! So what can I do to help you." That was not the response I expected. Jacob was such an anomaly for me. On the one hand, he was so calculating when it came to work and politics but so kind hearted and open about other things. I told him I just wanted him to know and I left his office feeling rather light hearted.

The challenge was my mother. She was dead set against the idea. Admittedly, she in principle had "agreed" on the basis that she had warned me, and that I was on my own. But that was a year ago. And since Bulk, the priesthood hadn't come up again. To go to her now and tell her I was actually going to begin the process of becoming a priest was bound to bring all the negativity that had for some time now subsided. But this was such a big decision for me and I was still so insecure a person that I needed approval from other people, especially from my mother. I decided to start with the other people and then work my way slowly to her.

I started with Margaret. I was very nervous about talking to her because if there was anyone who could bring my mother to the point of reason I thought she could. And if she didn't continue to support me, I would be truly alone. I was in the middle of a long drive when I felt the time was right to call her. So I took a deep breath and called. As soon as the phone started ringing, I went into a frantic plea to God asking that He should make sure she didn't answer the phone.

"Helloooooo!" She and I have a standing joke about the exaggerated way in which a mutual friend of ours answers the phone.

"Hey! how are you?" I asked trying to sound relaxed.

We exchanged pleasantries and talked for about ten minutes about random things. It was a very welcome "random things" conversation which I hoped would never end. But then she asked, "So what's up?"

"I've decided to apply for the priesthood." I just put it out there without adding any flowery language or explanation. And without missing a beat she said, "Oooh! This is very good news!" Her enthusiasm and excitement about the whole thing was almost anticlimactic, because I was so ready to explain myself.

So I jumped to plan B and said, "But Mummy is dead set against it."

"Of course she is! She's your mother and she's worried for you." At that point, I worked out what the situation was: while my mother would not find an ally in Margaret, she would find a source of comfort. I looked up to heaven and smiled at God. The 'sneaky Old Man' had clearly been working in the background while I was stressing.

> **Behold, I am going to send an angel before you to guard you along the way and to bring you into the place which I have prepared. Exodus 23:20 (NIV)**

It felt good that Margaret approved. But a few days later the fear of my mother's disapproval consumed me. So I called my brother. Being a total strategist, he looked at it purely from the standpoint of how it would benefit me. He and I had discussed this a year earlier but this time he seemed to take it seriously. I guess he realized that I had truly made up my mind. We did the analysis and concluded that overall, priesthood would be beneficial for my wellbeing. So he approved. But that was not the approval my heart needed. I needed my mother's blessing.

I called Sika. She, just like the last time I had called her about this, asked me a series of questions that revolved around me. How I felt and what I wanted to do. The emphasis was very much on me and not my mother or anyone else. In the end, she said to me again, "I think you should come in and see me." At the time, that was the most dissatisfying of all the conversations I had with anyone. She was forcing me to make a choice. To think based on what I wanted and not what other people would approve of. Again, I didn't recognize her voice as God trying to shine His light into a very dark place in my life, my sense of self-worth.

The depth of my insecurity was astounding. My job and my position and all the good things happening around me were a crutch. They made me feel like someone. But I myself within me could not stand on my own without them. And until I came to a place where I could see myself for who I am in Christ, I was always going to look for validation from other people and I would never be able to bring value to the priesthood. This I later came to recognize was the real reason why God held back the approval of my mother. To force me to confront myself. To remove all my crutches and give me nowhere else to look but to Him.

> **How can you believe since you accept glory from one another but do not seek the glory that comes from the only God? John 5:44 (NIV)**

The next crutch to go was my job. Reverend Idan called me out of the blue and said, "You need to leave Bulk and move on." I remember being particularly agitated by this call. *Move on to what?* I thought it was deeply insensitive of him to say that, especially since he knew I was a single parent, with a single income and was just coming out of what essentially had been poverty. I wrote him off as not being able to understand the corporate world. But he was actually the voice of God, that I again missed. A few weeks later my dear friend Kofi Boateng and I were having lunch when he said, "I really think you should leave Bulk, especially since it is an election year. If anything happens and this party loses, they will come for you."

"Come for me for what? I haven't done anything wrong." I knew I had no political affiliations, so that thought had quite frankly never crossed my mind. I was naïve.

"I know, but you are here in a very high position. No one believes you got this job on your own. If there is any kind of trouble, your name will be mixed up in it and your name is all you have."

These were all valid points but, seeing how he didn't offer to pay my daughter's school fees as he was dishing out free advice, I decided to dismiss it. And so once again, I shut out the voice of God.

Well maybe I heard it a bit, because some of these conversations kept me up at night for weeks afterwards. I called Sika to run it by her since she had actually done some consulting work for Bulk. Without missing a beat, she advised that based on what she had seen at Bulk, she believed I should put an exit plan together because Bulk was too toxic for me. She asked me to consider how many times I had complained to her about how there were so many things I disliked about Bulk. She also asked me to look in the mirror at how much weight I had gained and how my face was breaking out due to stress. I had never seen these things before. I had always been a small person and even though I was still smaller than most people, she was right. I had gained a significant amount of weight. I weighed more than I did when I was pregnant. That was shocking for me. I didn't realize how terrible my mental state had made me look.

That night, I wept and I asked God for guidance. By morning, it was clear to me that I needed to leave Bulk no matter what. I called Sika and told her of my plans to resign within the next six months. "Why six months?" She asked. "If you are sure you want to leave, leave now." I knew she was right. I was just stalling because I was afraid. Afraid of going back to not having money. Afraid of losing my new found approval from my family. I decided to revert back to my deal making with God. I prayed and I said to Him that since He had given me the job and He was now asking me to walk away, I would do so but on one condition. He needed to show me a sign, something that would give me comfort.

After I prayed, I wrote my resignation letter and went to bed. The next day, I turned it in. Jacob was stunned, which honestly surprised me because I had signaled him severally that I was unhappy. I guess he didn't realize I was unhappy enough to quit.

On my last day I went round the office and said goodbye to everyone. I went by Pierre's office to let him know that none of it was personal. I was hoping we could let bygones be bygones and have a good laugh. But he didn't seem to be in a laughing mood. He said goodbye coldly and that was it. I haven't seen him since.

That last time when I walked out of Bulk, I literally looked to heaven for my sign. Nothing came. Honestly, I don't know what I thought I would see but I believed God would show me something to assure me that I had made the right call. That evening, when the news had spread that I had quit Bulk, I received three job offers from a South African company, a British company and then a Ghanaian company in that order. That was my sign! I declined all three offers, went to the gym and paid up for a full year of membership.

CHAPTER TEN

BECOMING REVEREND

But you are a chosen people, a royal Priesthood, a holy nation, God's special possession, that you may declare the praises of him who called you out of darkness into his wonderful light.
1 Peter 2:9 (NIV)

GOD BREAKS PROTOCOL FOR US

The next six months of my life were what I can only describe as a fallow time in the life of farming land. I practically spent every day doing nothing but pray. But this time, it was a different kind of prayer. I did not need anything. I was perfectly happy to be unemployed. I was tired and stressed from Bulk and I needed a break. I spent my mornings at the gym and my afternoons praying. And in the evenings I ran. The difference with my prayers this time was that, it was as if my soul was crying out to God for company. I just had this deep and constant yearning to spend time with God. I guess God was preparing me mentally, spiritually, physically and emotionally for my new vocation of priesthood which path I was now fully committed to.

> **You, God, are my God, earnestly I seek you; I thirst for you, my whole being longs for you, in a dry and parched land where there is no water. Psalm 63:1 (NIV)**

All the hesitation and fear I felt seemed to fade away. My mother could see my resolve and we came to a point of agreeing to disagree. I later discovered that Canon Lamptey had sat her down and somehow gotten her to understand the burden I was feeling. He made her see that not even her protective love for me could ease what I felt in my heart from God. With that sorted, all I needed to do was begin the process of becoming a priest.

The Anglican Church has a well laid-out structure for priesthood and it is far more complex than I had imagined. The first stage involves telling your local parish priest of your intentions. The parish priest then sets up a committee, made up of members of your parish, whose job it is to assess you and determine your suitability as a priest. Essentially, they meet and talk about every aspect of your life as they know it and make a decision. Given my life so far, I already had doubts about how this was going to go. But God in His infinite wisdom had allowed the whole church and therefore by default this committee to listen to me as a preacher for at least two years. I was told later by someone in the committee that they were so delighted to see my name as a potential candidate for priesthood that the discussion revolved more around what had taken me so long, and not so much about whether or not I should be considered.

The next stage was for the committee to take that recommendation back to the parish priest who would then take it to the Bishop for consideration. The day Canon Lamptey took mine to the Bishop, he told me about it and even showed me the form he had filled. Within what seemed like a few short days, he brought me another form to fill and asked me to prepare for an interview with the Commission on Ministry. This is the Diocesan Committee that interviews people and determines their eligibility for priesthood.

I found the forms somewhat complex. The parts about my career and what I had done generally with my life were pretty simple. But I needed to prove that I was a baptized and confirmed Christian of sound mind. To do that I needed to find both my baptismal and confirmation certificates and I needed to find a mental health professional to clear me. And I only had two weeks to pull all this off.

Normally, this would not have been complicated except I was baptized a Presbyterian, by a priest who only made a note of my baptism in a book but never issued a certificate. And now he was dead. I didn't think it would be possible to track this note after almost forty years. But when I went to the Presbyterian Church of Ghana, they just went to their 1976 records, pulled out a book and there it was. I asked for a certificate to be issued which they agreed. But then, a cat and mouse game ensued, which essentially prevented me from ever picking up the certificate. I still don't have it.

The problem with my confirmation certificate was similar. I was confirmed as an Anglican, but for some reason, none of us in that batch of confirmands was given any certificate. I remember so clearly that for nearly five years after our confirmation, there was a particular lady who kept telling me how I needed to help her follow up on our certificates. As a seventeen-year-old at the time, what she was saying sounded like a lot of effort for very little reward, so I did nothing about it. Now here I was twenty-three years later, wishing I had taken her request more seriously.

My third problem was that I had no idea where to get a

mental health evaluation done. With all these obstacles to my interview to be considered for priesthood, it was clear to me that there was no way I could be ready for the interview which was now in two days' time. So I decided to fill the forms as best as I could and go in on the morning of the interviews to withdraw my name and sign up for the next interview session whenever it would be.

On the morning of the interviews, I went to the Diocesan office completely unprepared for the interview because I wasn't planning on being interviewed. Just as I approached the entrance lobby of the Bishop's Court to go and see the administrator, the Dean of the Cathedral called me from behind. I spun around and he said, "Your name came late but we have fitted you in so sit down in the waiting area, we will call you." I began a small protest and tried to let him know that my application form was not complete and that I didn't have all the documentation they were asking for. I don't think he heard me, or maybe he did and just chose to ignore me. Either way, he just kept walking and said firmly, "Sit in the waiting area we will call you."

Now I was petrified. What were they going to ask me? I didn't know the first five things about Anglicanism or priesthood or anything. What if they asked me my favorite Scripture? I knew a lot of Scripture because of all the preaching but I've always sought to understand and apply Scripture rather than to memorize it. So I have never been good at pin-pointing exactly where a given Scripture is. I walked into the waiting room and in there sat seven men. Three of them were in cassocks with a blue girdle, two were in cassocks with a black girdle and the other two were dressed in regular clothes. A girdle is the rope Anglican priests wear around their waist. It is a reminder to us as priests to gird our loins. As is written in 1 Peter 1:13-15, "Therefore gird up the loins of your mind, be sober, and rest your hope fully upon the grace that is to be brought to you at the revelation of Jesus Christ; as obedient children, not conforming yourselves to the former lusts, as in your ignorance; but as He who called you is holy, you also be holy in all your conduct."

I discovered that day that when the Bishop approves your bid for priesthood you become what is known as an ordinand. As an ordinand, you have no priestly duties and your primary role is to watch the priest who is discipling you and learn primarily by observation.

This is how you learn about the traditions and practices of the Anglican Church and Anglican priests. You learn about the order of service, giving communion and other practices that are unique to the Anglican Church that you wouldn't have learnt in seminary. Those were the guys in the cassock with a blue girdle. That office if you can call it that, lasts for about a year. After which you are interviewed by this same committee and upon approval by them and the Bishop, you are ordained a deacon.

A deacon is the first level of priesthood and at that level, the only sacrament you can perform is Baptism. Those were the guys in the black girdle. That office also lasts at least a year after which you are interviewed again. If you get through that interview and the Bishop approves, then you are ordained a priest. This is the second level of priesthood, and at this level you can give communion, perform weddings, funerals and other sacraments except ordination and confirmation. Those two sacraments are the preserve of the Bishop alone. The Bishop is the third level of priesthood.

With this vast gap in my knowledge, I listened to these men who were also scheduled for the interview throw questions at each other, "List the seasons of the Anglican calendar in order, starting with Easter?" "What are the colors for each season and how long does each one last?" "List five canons of the Anglican Church." "What is the Sursum Corda?" I had no idea what any of these things were! Clearly priesthood required a lot more than delivering sermons and I simply was not ready for it. But I was in the room and walking away was clearly not an option, so I decided to learn, at least as much as I could.

Suddenly, the door burst open and a stocky gentleman walked in. He was not in a cassock but I could tell from his collar that he was a priest. "We will be calling you in this order; deacons, ordinands and then the rest of you." We all quieted down. "When your interview is over, walk out, and don't speak to anyone. Okay?" "You!" He said pointing to one of the men in a black girdle, "you are first!" And with that, it was on. The gentleman got up, adjusted his girdle and straightened out his cassock. He took a deep breath and stepped out of the waiting area.

The rest of us continued to discuss in hushed tones. Fifteen minutes later, he walked out, silent and expressionless. I didn't know what to make of it. My stomach was tied into a huge knot as I sat and watched all the deacons and ordinands emerge with no expression. Then the first regular guy was called, his name was Richard. I somehow knew I was next. I wished I was not but every fiber in my body said I was. I waited eagerly for him to emerge. And emerge he did, with a hurried gait, visibly upset and with the comment, "This whole thing is a joke!" The last gentleman and I stared blankly at each other. *This is not good*, I thought. My thought had barely settled in my head when I heard my name, "Ms. Ofori-Boateng."

I took a deep breath and walked in. I was dressed for a corporate interview and as I walked in with my heels clicking, I wondered if that was the way I should have come. "Have a seat."

the Dean said with a warm smile. I knew him reasonably well
and he had worked extensively with my mother on several church
legal issues. So I felt I had an ally in the room. The room was
arranged in a u-shape with a chair at the open end. Very much
like my seminary interview. Maybe it is a holy thing. Who knows!
There were somewhere between eight and nine people in the
room. I recognized two of them as priests apart from the Dean
but the others I didn't know. Two of them were women and I had
read that some of the greatest opponents to female ordination
were women, so I was not sure if having women on the panel
would serve me well or not.

The first question was from one of the ladies, "Why do you
want to be a priest?"

I thought about blurting out, "I don't want to be a priest!"
But that didn't seem like wisdom. So I began to recount the story
I have told up until this point. I cried throughout the narration.
So much so that the other lady kept asking if I was okay and if I
needed a break. The first lady seemed annoyed that I was crying.
Almost as if she felt I was letting the side down.

When I was done, they gave me some time to calm down
and then dug into the technical questions that I was so petrified
of. I didn't know the answers to most of them. They asked me
what a Paschal Candle was. The word candle gave it away but
beyond being a candle I couldn't tell them much. I didn't even
know what my favorite Scripture was. I was able to say the
Scripture but I could not tell where it was in a Bible. In case you
wondered, its 1 Corinthians 2:9 which says, "However, as it is
written: What no eye has seen, what no ear has heard and what
no human mind has conceived -- the things God has prepared for
those who love him." That day, it became very evident to me that
I had completely misunderstood and underrated what it takes to

become a priest and I needed to go back to engineering and leave the difficult work of priesthood to real professionals. I left feeling disappointed. Very disappointed in myself for failing God.

That afternoon my phone rang. It was the Dean, "Akua, you did so well, the committee was really impressed with you. We are recommending you for priesthood. The Bishop's office will call you." To this day, I still cannot understand what they saw or heard in there. Not only did I not have a completed application form with the necessary supporting documents, I was unprepared and I didn't know even the most fundamental aspects of our faith. Yet somehow, this team of priests and scholarly men and women were impressed with my answers. For me, it was confirmation that when God decides on a path for our lives, He will make it happen no matter what obstacles we put in the way. Even if the obstacle is ourselves, our own foolishness or insufficiency, He will set us aside, break all protocol and make sure that His will is done.

> **And He has said to me, "My grace is sufficient for you, for power is perfected in weakness." Most gladly, therefore, I will rather boast about my weaknesses, so that the power of Christ may dwell in me. Therefore, I am well content with weaknesses, with insults, with distresses, with persecutions, with difficulties, for Christ's sake; for when I am weak, then I am strong. 2 Corinthians 12:9-10 (NIV)**

A week later the Bishop's office did indeed call and set up an appointment for me to have a one-on-one meeting with him.

I had never met the Bishop before. I caught a glimpse of him the day he was made Bishop. I had seen him several times since at a distance but he always looked so stern. So I assumed he was a stern person and I didn't want to mess up. I went to review some stuff about Anglicanism and made sure I actually knew where my favorite verse in the Bible was in case he asked.

His office was upstairs and required you to walk through a few doors before you arrived at his door. I imagined it was like what the Jewish priests had to go through to get to the Holy of Holies. When I arrived, I waited in his outer lobby for about ten minutes, then I was advanced to his inner lobby. After about another ten minutes or so, his secretary, a distinguished looking elderly gentleman, nodded at me and said in a whisper that I should knock. I knocked on the door so softly that I barely heard it myself but the Bishop answered immediately, "Come in."

It was a medium-sized room with wood paneling on the walls and wine wall-to-wall carpeting. The whole room seemed very holy and royal at the same time, with large Victorian style chairs. "Sister Akua, have a seat" he offered very cheerfully. That was surprising! Surprising in a nice way. I sat and we had the most normal everyday chat one can think of. He asked about my mother, my daughter, work, and life in general. The only thing he asked about priesthood was if I spoke any local language fluently. Apparently, he needed that information to determine where to post me. And that was it, he ended the conversation by saying, "Go and buy yourself a white cassock and a blue girdle." He saw the excitement in my face and suppressed his own smile. Then dismissed me.

TO SERVE GOD IS TO SERVE MAN

I was giddy with excitement. I called my mother, who offered to buy me lunch as a reward. And then I called Canon Lamptey. It is important that I point out here that I owed that day and indeed every day of my priesthood to Canon Lamptey. It was through his listening with humility to God that I ever had the chance to preach at St. Anthony. Him relinquishing his pulpit to me was the true turning point in my life. I find it extraordinary that he would give up his pulpit for a complete novice and be thrilled as I excelled. I'll hazard a guess and say there are very few people who would do that for another person.

Thanks to him, the first day I preached as an ordinand at the Holy Trinity Cathedral, where I was posted, I handled it like a pro. That day, several well-wishing parishioners came to me with pointers and encouragement, telling me not to be nervous and to just keep it simple. I'm sure they were surprised at how easily I took it all. They had no idea I had been honing my skills for the last two years at St Anthony. Later that morning, I saw the Most Reverend Dr. Ofei and said to him excitedly, "I preached today!" To which he said, "Oh. But you've been preaching for a long time now." That was when I realized the true magnitude of what Canon Lamptey had done. He had allowed me two years to mess up at his pulpit despite the fact that I was neither a deacon nor a priest. I was not even an ordinand.

Being an ordinand was humbling. If I translate it into corporate terms, the ordinand in the church setting is the equivalent of the errand boy. It carries no glory and everyone knows you are clueless. The servers lord their knowledge over you and each day you are in church, it hits you how little you know.

I often juxtaposed it against my role at Bulk, where as soon as my car pulled up, someone rushed to open the door, another person asked to carry my bags and a third person started making enquiries about whether I wanted tea or coffee and if I had any idea what I wanted for lunch. I would often get into a tussle with the person who wanted to carry my bags, because I don't like my bags to be carried for me, especially my handbag. I was used to people fussing over me at work. But at church, I was the definition of a minion.

Nobody did anything for me. I had to carry my own things and find my own coffee. But I loved it. This contrast was necessary for me and I believe God orchestrated it that way to drum home the point that the path He was taking me on, was a path that required me to submit totally to His will. I loved the whole environment of church. It gave me the peace I had experienced as a teenager all those years ago when I used to run off to the Cathedral. And I loved the feeling of being in service to God.

> **Whoever exalts himself will be humbled and whoever humbles himself will be exalted. Matthew 23:12 (NIV)**

The priest in whose care I was put for mentoring and discipleship was an incredible teacher. He and I established a weekly meeting where he would teach me about Anglicanism. He taught me about the meanings of all the vestments we wear, showed me the Scriptures accompanying them as well as all the Scriptures that are used for every ritual we perform. I discovered that there is nothing random about Anglicanism. Everything is carefully scripted to align with the Word of God and can be supported by it.

About three months into my stewardship as an ordinand, the priest mentoring me told me that during the debate over female priesthood, he had been one of the loudest voices against it. I was stunned by this revelation. I had never actually met a person who was against female ordination, although I knew many people were. When I asked how he had overcome it, he said, he was under canonical obedience to the Bishop and therefore once the Bishop had decreed it, he accepted it and has not questioned it since. This was a huge eye opener for me. It made me see that service to God is about being completely selfless.

> **I can do nothing on my own initiative. Just as I hear, I judge and my judgment is just, because I do not seek my own will but the will of the one who sent me. John 5:30 (NIV)**

I reflected deeply on this conversation with my mentor and his attitude, and decided I needed to be more disciplined and selfless. I needed to park some of my preconceived notions about people and situations. I needed to truly seek out the will of God, whether or not I agreed with it, and execute it to the best of my ability.

After a year as an ordinand, I was called into my second interview with the Commission on Ministry. This time, there were fewer tears and three of us were selected for ordination. Two men would become priests and I would become a deacon.

Part of the process of getting ordained is going into retreat with your fellow candidates and with what is called a Retreat Conductor. Since there were only three of us, we retreated at the Bishop's Court. Our Retreat Conductor was Reverend Canon Samuel Gyabi Danquah. He died a few months after we were ordained. May he rest in peace.

For the week that we were in retreat, we interacted with no one except each other and the lady who brought us food. We spent the time in deep study, prayer and worship. Each morning we woke up at the crack of dawn for morning Mass. After that, we would pray and meditate before breakfast. The rest of the day was split between learning about priesthood and just being quiet. In fact, the whole retreat was a study in silence. We only spoke in hushed tones at meal times as was necessary and when we needed to ask our Retreat Conductor a question.

During this retreat, I came to understand that by accepting to go down the path of priesthood, I was opening up my life to public scrutiny. Many of the things that I could do and say in public and get away with, would no longer fly. Canon Gyabi Danquah used the example of flying off the handle at someone in public. It all seemed so unfair and I, as the only ordinand, was particularly vocal about it. But he showed me in Scripture that becoming Reverend is far more about self-sacrifice, not only for God but also for man. And part of that self-sacrifice is living a life that will not cause anyone to stumble on your account.

It was at that retreat, that I came to fully understand what Ambily meant when she said you can't love God and hate man. They are one and the same. To love God and serve Him is to love and serve your neighbor. Christ understood this to the point where He sacrificed everything including His own life just so that we, His brothers and sisters, would not be condemned.

> **So then, let us pursue what leads to peace and to mutual edification. Do not destroy the work of God for the sake of food. All food is clean but it is wrong for a man to let his eating be a stumbling block. It is better not to eat meat or drink wine or to do anything to cause your brother to stumble. Romans 14:20-21 (NIV)**

I found a brand new sense of purpose in this retreat. Up until then, my idea of priesthood had been about service to God. And about my relationship with Him. I was so focused on how much I could sacrifice for Him, that I failed to see that He Himself does not require my sacrifice. I began to understand that my priesthood and indeed my life needed to be about doing for others, about service to man, about looking deep within myself and pulling out what God has deposited in there for the benefit of other people. I suddenly realized that all the difficulties I had been through in life were never about me or for my edification.

The purpose of all my pain and my suffering was to serve and encourage others faced with the same or similar situations for the purposes of edifying God.

> **I want you to show love, not offer sacrifice. I want you to know me more than I want burnt offerings. Hosea 6:6 (NIV)**

This epiphany left me wondering how I could have been an ordinand in God's church for a year and yet it was the week of my ordination into the diaconate that He truly began to break down my ego and teach me to get past myself. I began to feel even more unworthy of priesthood than I had felt before. The night before the ordination, I sat alone in my room and wept. I asked God to confirm for me that He was sure He wanted me to be a priest. I prayed in earnest but nothing happened. God was silent.

Now that I think about it, my sign was the breaking I was feeling within myself. The fact that I realized just how unworthy I was and indeed still am, was all that God wanted me to see.

> **Be grateful for your sins - they are carriers of grace. Anthony De Mello**

The next day, we were all up at the crack of dawn and vested in silence. When we arrived at the church, we were ushered into the vestry, where our Bishop and a few other Bishops from other diocese were gathered. It was nice to see other people and be able to talk a little more, albeit still in hushed tones.

THE GOD WHO STARTS IT, WILL ACCOMPLISH IT

The ceremony itself was very sobering. To begin with, we had to process into the church in a very specific order. Anglicans are very particular about the order of procession. So after we prayed, all close to fifty of us arranged ourselves in this particular order and walked solemnly into the church:

Verger

Thurifer and Boat Boy

Acolytes and Cross Bearer

Torch Bearers

Wardens

Master of Ceremonies

Deacon and Sub Deacon

Canons

Arch Deacons

Dean

Bishop's Chaplain

Bishop

Chancellor

Registrar

Assistant Registrar

Retreat Conductor (Preacher for the day)

Deacons

Ordinands

As the only ordinand, I brought up the rear.

Once we had all genuflected before the altar and settled into our seats, the Mass proceeded like it would on a normal Sunday. Then after the reading of the Epistle, the Bishop moved to sit directly in front of the altar and the choir began to sing a hymn which began with the words;

Lord, pour thy Spirit from on high,
And thine ordained servants bless;
Graces and gifts to each supply,
And clothe thy Priests with righteousness.

I remember thinking to myself that maybe if God clothed me in righteousness, I wouldn't feel like such an imposter.

The hymn ended.

And in a loud voice, the Dean said, "Let those to be made deacons approach." He motioned the congregation to sit and as I listened to the heave of over five hundred people sit, I took a deep breath and stood. It had seemed very cool at first that I was the only person to be ordained a deacon that day but at that moment, as I had to stand alone, I wished there had been another person with me.

Then the Dean said, "Reverend Father in God, we present to you this person who is to be ordained to the office of deacon in the Church of God."

"Has she been selected in accordance with the Canons and the Ordination Process of this Church? And do you believe her manner of life to be suitable to the exercise of this ministry?" Asked the Bishop.

As I stood there, the gravity of the whole process kept washing over me. I had always lived my life for me, as I pleased. And now that life, which I assumed was mine to do what I wanted with, was being looked at as if it belonged to someone else. But I guess that was and is the whole point. Our lives don't belong to us. Our bodies are not ours to do with as we please. They belong to God and whenever He chooses, He can call upon us to answer for what we have done with them. That day, I cringed thinking about some of the things I had done in my life, but almost instantaneously the

Holy Spirit reminded me that while we were still sinners, Christ died for us. And by that death, He made every single one of us clean and whole. That is the promise Christ has made to each of us and no matter what we have done, it is a promise we must cling to. We cannot and must not allow anyone, not even our own self, to ever make us feel like we have sinned beyond the redemption of Jesus.

The Dean responded, "We certify to you that she has satisfied the requirements of the Canons and the Ordination Process of the Diocese and we believe her to be qualified for this Order."

The Bishop motioned me to turn and face the congregation. I turned and looked straight at my mother. She had on a complete poker face but her eyes were full of pride. I felt like smiling so I quickly looked away as the Bishop said, "Those whose duty it is to enquire about this person and examine her have found her to be of godly life and sound learning and believe her to be duly called to serve God in her ministry. Is it therefore your will that she should be ordained?"

In unison, the congregation said, "It is."

Then he asked, "Will you uphold her in her ministry?"

Again in unison the congregation said, "We will."

With that, I turned again to face the Bishop, genuflected and walked over to the Chancellor, the lawyer for the Diocese, who handed me a Bible. With that Bible in hand, I swore an oath to uphold the laws of the church in executing my duties as a deacon. I also swore an oath of canonical obedience to the Bishop and all other Bishops after him. I signed against these oaths and was led back to my seat by the Master of Ceremonies. But that was not the ordination. That was the legal part. The ordination proper, the God part, was yet to happen. But for now, it was the turn of the two gentlemen to be made priests to complete the legal part of their ceremony.

When they were done, they both genuflected and turned to walk toward the Western door. That is the entrance directly opposite the Altar. As they went past me, I stood and joined behind them in march step and all three of us made the walk through the aisle to the door where three wooden crosses lay waiting for us to carry on our shoulder back to the Altar. Within the Anglican Church in Accra, this is the highlight of ordination and the church is always very spiritually charged.

We had rehearsed this as part of our retreat the week before and when I carried my cross, I wondered why during the actual ordinations I had seen, the candidates seemed to struggle so much to carry their crosses. Because in all honesty, they are not heavy at all. But that day, something was different. When I went to pick up my cross, I could hardly lift it. It is difficult to explain because physically, it was still very light but once I put it on my shoulder and the whole church wailed the hymn;

> *Take up thy cross, the Saviour said,*
> *If thou wouldst My disciple be;*
> *Deny thyself, the world forsake,*
> *And humbly follow after Me.*

I couldn't move under the weight of the cross.

I wasn't sure what to do. The words of the hymn, mingled with the shrieks of people as they were slain in the Spirit was overwhelming. Surely I couldn't put the cross down and walk away. The order of returning to the altar was reversed. This meant I was now in front, leading the procession with the two to be made priests behind me. I knew I had to find a way to make the now seemingly eternal walk down the aisle to the Altar with my back almost doubled over from the weight of this unbearable cross.

The Master of Ceremonies came up beside me and whispered, "let's go!" I took a step. And then another. As I walked, I prayed the same prayer over and over and over, "God, please, please, please help me with this cross." As I prayed tears rolled down my face uncontrollably. And all the time, the wailing and the hymn continued;

> *Take up thy cross, nor heed the shame,*
> *Nor let thy foolish pride rebel;*
> *Thy Lord for thee the Cross endured,*
> *To save thy soul from death and hell.*

With each step towards the Altar, I pondered over the words of the hymn and the cross got heavier. I held onto it tighter for fear that I might drop it. The edges of the cross dug into my palm and it hurt but there was no way I was going to let go.

At last, I got to the Altar. Someone came up behind me and took away the cross. We all knelt and then lay prostrate before the Altar. While we lay there, the rest of the church knelt and the Litanist, began to sing the Litany of Ordination. It was beautiful! His voice was angelic. With each line he chanted, the congregation responded, "Lord, hear our prayer."

And I wept.

At some point during the chant, the Bishop took over and sang the words, "Bless these thy servants and handmaid, ordinand chosen to be deacon, and deacons chosen to be priests, in your Church and pour your grace upon them, we pray to you, O Lord." As the congregation responded, I felt a coldness pour over me. It was the same coldness I had felt when Ambily first taught me how to pray. I smiled to myself and thought, *"Wow! Ambily's Jesuú is here!"*

Later that night I sent Ambily a video clip of the cross bearing part of the ordination on WhatsApp. She wrote back the words, "I praise God for your life. I always knew you were a special one."

When the litany was over, we were asked to kneel and one after the other the Bishop laid hands on us and ordained us. As the only ordinand to be made a deacon, I went first. He laid hands on me and blessed me. He gave me a Bible as a sign of my duty to read and properly translate Scripture.

Do your best to present yourself to God as one approved, a worker who does not need to be ashamed and who correctly handles the word of truth. 2 Timothy 2:15 (NIV)

Then he gave me a stole to wear across my left shoulder as a sign of Christ's yoke which I was to take on in exchange for my burdens.

Take my yoke upon you and learn from me, for I am gentle and humble in heart and you will find rest for your souls. For my yoke is easy and my burden is light. Matthew 11:29-30 (NIV)

And with that I became Reverend.

CHAPTER ELEVEN

BE MY GUARDIAN AND MY GUIDE

I became a servant of this gospel by the gift of God's grace given me through the working of his power. Although I am less than the least of all the Lord's people, this grace was given me: to preach to the Gentiles the boundless riches of Christ.
Ephesians 3:7 (NIV)

After I became a deacon, I was posted back to the Holy Trinity Cathedral. But this time as Reverend Akua. I struggled with the title because it carried with it a reverence and a grace that I simply did not feel.

"What do you think being Reverend should feel like?" Sika asked.

The question startled me. I had never thought about it. I was so obsessed with this feeling of unworthiness that I had not bothered to process what she asked.

"Holy, I guess." I answered feeling foolish.

In my hiatus from work, I had come to agree with Sika that I did indeed need counselling to help me get past my pain and shame. I had been seeing her for a few months before I was ordained a deacon. And now that I was a deacon, I was struggling with guilt from my past and this incessant feeling that I was a fraud. That I was unworthy to have been chosen for ordination. I struggled so much so that I was embarrassed to tell anyone that

I was a deacon. I believed that I was not by any standard what anyone would call a true representation of an Anglican priest, or any representative of Christ. After all, I was a divorced, single parent.

I was convinced that the fact that I was not married, or more specifically divorced, probably disqualified me in people's eyes when it came to priesthood. I suppose it didn't help when one day, I was at a hospital, when a clergywoman from the Baptist church chastised me and the whole Anglican church for ordaining a divorced person. Her exact words to me were, "I don't want to be part of a church that ordains divorced people." I was so deeply affected by this comment, that the next time I saw Sika, I tried to use it as justification for why I needed to hide my priesthood. Sika again pushed me to look within me and find what it was that was bothering me about what the lady had said. Honestly, I searched hard and all I could find was that I myself believed that I was not good enough for God. All I could feel was shame and darkness about this one blotch in my life.

BROKEN

But that day, God was bent on bringing me into the light and He used Sika to do it. She asked me one question which created a massive shift in me. She said, "I know you think it's humility to feel unworthy of the office you have received but have you considered that it is pride to think that you can ever be worthy of that office?" It struck me like a blow to my stomach. Here I was, so fixated on my past sins and how I needed to try and overcome them, that despite all my theological training and even my ordination, I did not recognize that Christ had already died for me and cleansed me. I was so caught up in the lie that I needed to do something to be worthy that I could not move forward. That belief in such lies is precisely where the devil wants us. So stuck on a cycle of guilt and shame that we cannot see our way clear to execute God's purpose in our lives.

> **The thief comes only to steal and kill and destroy; I have come that they may have life and have it to the full. John 10:10 (NIV)**

The truth is, it does not matter what we have done, where we have been, what we have said, or even how negatively people perceive us because of our past. Once we commit ourselves to God, literally deny self, take up our cross and follow Him, He is more than able to use us in ways that are far beyond our wildest dreams. That path does not have to be about priesthood. God calls all of us for different assignments. For me, it is priesthood. But it could have been anything; teaching, medical practice, legal practice, sports, writing; anything! The important thing is that we must have the humility to realize that we will never be worthy of His call. And in as much as we are not worthy of that call, He will equip us to execute the call. However, in that equipping process, He will break us, remold us, transform us and get rid of any aspect of our being that cannot serve His purpose. He had to break my bitterness, my vengefulness, my insecurity, my pride and my addiction to other people's approval, in order to use me.

> **Do not conform to the pattern of this world but be transformed by the renewing of your mind. Then you will be able to test and approve what God's will is. Romans 12:2 (NIV)**

My desire to look good and righteous in the eyes of everyone, to appear as if I have a perfect past, or at best be apologetic for my past had robbed me of my ability to love myself. It had rendered me unable to control my own behavior, my own emotions and my own thoughts. Rather, I reflected the behaviors, emotions and thoughts of other people in an effort to please them and get their approval.

God has created each of us in His image, as whole and complete human beings. And into each of us, He has deposited all the abilities and strengths that we need to thrive on this Earth. Of all these abilities probably the most important one is the ability to love ourselves and to respond to the world around us based not on how the world says we should respond but based on our own acknowledgement of who we are in Christ. When we are sure of our identity in Christ and convinced that God has created us as a special person then, we will stop seeking guidance in what other people think we should do, or should be, or should have at any given stage in life. That constant seeking for the approval of the world can become a great source of distress.

The idea, of course, is not to discount or disregard all advice. Rather, it is to measure and weigh advice within the boundaries of who Christ is and who we are in Him. In other words, if we set God and not man as our True North, we can never be misguided by the opinions of our friends, family, our 'Man of God,' or anyone else. Had I known this, I would not have made the mistakes I made in my life. But nonetheless I feel grateful.

> **In everything give thanks; for this is the will of God in Christ Jesus for you. 1Thessalonians 5:18 (NKJV)**

FIRST COMES SELF-DISCOVERY...

Those first few months of counselling with Sika was like the unveiling of the full picture of the first forty years of my life. And as I watched the picture unfold in each session with her, I cried a lot. I saw a picture of a girl who, like the people of Israel, started out in the light and descended into a wilderness that she could not comprehend. And yet in that wilderness, God walked with me, carried me, fed me and protected me. Even when I was ready to deny and denounce Him, He was there. And even though I still had so much wrong with me, He anointed me a deacon. Not because of who I was, or what I had done but because of who He is and what He has done.

That was the lesson He wanted me to learn, that I never had, never did and never would have, or do anything that would make me worthy of Him. It was only when I learned that lesson that I came to a point of true humility and to a place where I could now say confidently that I am ordained, not of my doing but by the doing of the Lord.

> **Remember how the LORD your God led you all the way in the wilderness these forty years, to humble and test you in order to know what was in your heart, whether or not you would keep his commands. Deuteronomy 8:2 (NIV)**

...THEN RESTORATION

One afternoon after a session with Sika, I saw a WhatsApp message from Jürgen which read, "I'd like for us to have lunch, let me know what day will work. Pick your favorite restaurant." I was truly surprised, because my last interaction with Jürgen had been on the day of Jacob's press conference, when he called and threatened to sue Bulk at large and me in particular. I didn't know what to make of his message but at this stage in my life, I had gone beyond guessing and speculating. So I asked God. I drove to a Catholic Church nearby called Mary Mother of Good Counsel, parked my car, walked in and sat. Immediately, I felt the calm that I have come to know and experience in every church that is truly of God. And then I asked God, "What does Jürgen want?"

His response was swift. He showed me that Jürgen wanted to offer me a job and then told me to take the offer. It had been six months since I had left Bulk and at that time I had been offered a total of five jobs all of which I was clearly instructed to decline. But all of a sudden, God wanted me to take this job. Although God and I still had and have our disagreements, I had learned to trust Him, or more accurately, I had learned to trust that I was hearing Him correctly. Right there from my pew in the empty church, I sent Jürgen a message, with a location for us to have lunch.

A week later, we had lunch and before we ordered our meal, Jürgen offered me the Country Manager role of a global engineering company, earning the equivalent of what I would have earned if I had stayed in the USA and continued to build my career. I was completely blown away by the offer. It was as if God wanted me to know that He could and would restore all that I had lost by virtue of my divorce and everything that surrounded it. If I had known on the day of the press conference that the unpleasant call I received from Jürgen would later result in my dream job, I would have encouraged him to rip into me more than he actually did!

After our lunch, I drove back to Mary Mother of Good Counsel Catholic Church to thank God. And as I prayed, He reminded me of the message He had sent me over five years earlier through Darnell; Matthew 6:33 "Seek first his kingdom and his righteousness and all these things will be given to you as well." My goodness! He was right! And I remembered that Darnel had said to me, "I think He means seek His heart first and He will give you everything in His hands." Now it was all coming together for me. God all along just wanted me and indeed wants all of us to be fully committed to Him. He has no desire to withhold any good thing from any of us. But all our good things must come from Him otherwise we run the risk of thinking we own ourselves and our own pride will consume us.

> **So I will restore to you the years that the swarming locust has eaten...You shall eat in plenty and be satisfied. Joel 2:25-26 (NKJV)**

God indeed restored my life not just in material things but He restored me emotionally, mentally, physically and spiritually. He restored my being and gave me life. Not just eternal life but a life on earth to look forward to and be excited about. A life with purpose. From my experience, I learned that when we give our lives to Christ, truly give it to Him, the first thing He does is strip us of anything that He didn't give us. But because He is faithful and true, He will rebuild us and restore us beyond what we could ever have imagined.

To set up and run a foreign backed engineering firm in Ghana had always been a dream for me. I'll even hazard a guess and say it is the dream of many a returnee to live in Ghana and set up a company in their field of study, backed by the parent company, with the potential of creating a real legacy. Maybe I'm just unambitious but that had been my ideal returnee status and now, one sushi lunch later, it was my reality. I had believed in my heart that I would never practice as an engineer again and now I could spend half my time practicing what I had studied in school and the other half doing what I loved the most: public speaking. Only this time, truly meaningful public speaking, from behind

God's pulpit.

> **Know therefore that the LORD your God, He is God, the faithful God, who keeps His covenant and His loving kindness to a thousandth generation with those who love Him and keep His commandments. Deuteronomy 7:9 (NIV)**

PRIESTHOOD

Roughly six months after I delved into my Country Manager role, my mentor and teacher, the priest grooming me for priesthood, informed me that the time had come for me to be interviewed and assessed for ordination into the priesthood.

This time, I walked into the interview room prepared for what I thought I would be asked. After serving as a deacon for close to a year, I knew the Anglican Mass inside out. I knew how to chant all the major canticles and prefaces. I even knew what the Pascal Candle was! And I had several verses of Scripture that I could quote at the drop of a hat.

So with my white cassock and black girdle, I drove to Accra Ridge Church where the interviews were being held and sat in the waiting area. When I was called in, the very first question blew me away, "Why do you want to be a priest?" *What? I thought we had been through this!!* I never imagined they would ask me that again, but there I was, unprepared. Again! With what felt like God smiling in the background.

This time, however, I didn't cry. I told them my story over again, added the new bits and said to them that although I started out not wanting to be a priest, I had now come to a place of accepting that it is my true calling and that I was excited at the opportunity to serve. I think I convinced them, because they then delved into the technical questions that I was so ready for. I sang the Sursum Corda and one of the prefaces. In fact, they cut me off mid preface as if to say, since we can't fail you here let's move on to something that we can penalize you on. With that, I was asked to sing the *Libera Me*. It is the Latin for *Deliver Me* and is a responsorial sung at funerals to absolve the dead. I didn't know it.

Again God reminded me of humility in that interview. As soon as I admitted that I didn't know how to sing it, one of the panelist said, "As an Anglican priest, you will have to learn it." With that, they congratulated me and dismissed me. Again, it was when I was weak, when I didn't know, that God made me stand out and shine.

The ordination was a few weeks later and as usual, we were quarantined for a week. This time there were fifteen of us to be ordained. Fourteen guys and me.

For our retreat, we went to the Anglican retreat center, all fifteen of us and our Retreat Conductor, Canon Neequaye, now Dean of the Cathedral. Again, the only time I saw another woman in that week was when we were served food.

That retreat had a very different effect on me from the one before. In this one, I was sure of my calling. I was also very sure of my unworthiness and comfortable with it. My constant prayer was that God would fill me with His Holy Spirit and through Him, allow me to serve His church to the best of my ability. Incidentally, Dean Neequaye began each morning by having us sing the hymn *Come Holy Ghost our Hearts inspire*. It is a hymn that is sung by the Bishop at various official ceremonies of the church including ordination and the first verse is always sang by him alone.

The last line of the first verse of the hymn, is a prayer asking God to impart His sevenfold giftings of wisdom, understanding, counsel, fortitude, knowledge, piety and fear of the Lord onto us.

During our retreat those gifting of the Holy Spirit manifested very strongly. As all sixteen of us soaked ourselves in God, the Holy Spirit manifested differently in each of us. There were two guys in particular, with gifts that seemed so profound to me, probably because they are gifts that I just don't have in me.

The first gentleman was a tall, lean man with a voice like an angel. He sang so effortlessly and without being asked, became the natural leader for each day's praise and worship session. And when he would sing this particular hymn, we could all feel the Holy Spirit indeed come down to inspire each of our souls and deposit gifts into our beings. The second gentleman could pray so spontaneously and so profoundly that it was as if he had an insight into what was going on in each of our lives.

During the retreat, we discussed our faith and our role as priests. When I was ordained a deacon, we talked about these things but now that I would be a priest, the weight of my life, especially the fact that my life would no longer be completely private really registered. Now all of us would have to serve as a good example to society, often called to sacrifice our own human tendencies and desires for the purposes of our faith. As we shared with each other experiences of priesthood and church, I was struck by how difficult it was to incorporate the feminization of priesthood. Every example was in relation to male specific struggles. It didn't bother me at all. I just thought it was interesting. But it would begin a series of questions in my mind about the extent to which clergywomen have truly been incorporated into priesthood not just in the Anglican Church but in the church globally.

On the morning of our ordination into the priesthood, I woke up feeling light and happy. I knew it would be an emotional day for me because I could see just how far God had brought me.

I felt like I had been given a new lease of life. A second chance. I wondered the night before, where I would be if I had died in all my hate and bitterness and revenge. I didn't want to hazard a guess. But it put in me, a burning desire to share with other people just how loving and forgiving God is. If a base sinner like me could be on the verge of ordination in the order of Melchizedek, the order of Christ Himself, then certainly, no one has sinned beyond the salvation of God.

THE POWER OF PRAYER

That morning, I was the first to be ordained. When I was ordained a deacon, I was given a Bible and a stole. As a priest, a chasuble was placed over my vestments as a sign of the love and charity that must cover all that I do.

> **And over all these virtues put on love, which binds them all together in perfect unity. Colossians 3:14 (NIV)**

Then my hands were anointed.

> **And you shall anoint them and ordain them and consecrate them, that they may serve Me as Priests. Exodus 28:41 (NIV)**

After the Bishop had laid hands on us, he asked the congregation to pray. He said, "Let us pray, dearly beloved, to God the Father Almighty, that He would increase upon these servants and handmaid, now called to the order of priesthood, the gifts of His heavenly grace, that the work which, by His mercy, He has begun, may by His assistance be joyfully fulfilled through Jesus Christ Our Lord. Amen."

It seemed like a simple enough request. But when I heard

the heave of over one thousand people kneel down and pray, God used that moment to disabuse me of this notion I had, that praying for other people is not effective. I don't know what each person prayed but I do know that when it was over, I felt readier than ever to embark on this God trip. And with that, the organist struck the chord for that beautiful hymn that we had been singing all week and the Bishop on his own sang the words;

> *Come, Holy Ghost, our souls inspire,*
> *And lighten with celestial fire;*
> *Thou the anointing Spirit art,*
> *Who dost Thy sevenfold gifts impart;*

And pray in the Spirit on all occasions with all kinds of prayers and requests. With this in mind, be alert and always keep on praying for all the Lord's people. Ephesians 6:18 (NIV)

THIS IS MY THANK YOU

The next day, as is the tradition within the Anglican church in Accra, I celebrated my first Mass at my home parish, St Anthony of Padua, in a suburb of Accra call Abelenkpe. I preached to the hymn *Be Thou My Guardian and My Guide*. Using that hymn, I made a plea to each person seated there to be my guardian and my guide as I embarked on my priesthood journey. And in as much as it is still a very young journey, I would like to use this book to thank the various people who up until this point have helped me be the priest I am today.

I'll start with Fred Sam for making me aware that people are always watching me. Even as a parishioner, he was paying enough attention to notice that I would walk out of church immediately after communion. It has taught me that, now more than ever, people are watching me. And so for the sake of Christ, I cannot afford to go down the wrong path lest I lead others astray.

> **Woe to the world for temptations to sin! For it is necessary that temptations come but woe to the one by whom the temptation comes! Matthew 18:7 (NIV)**

I'm grateful to Mr. George Oppong, Mrs. Evelyn Lamptey, the late Professor John S. Pobee, the late Bishop Dadson and the Late Pastor Kofi Awadzie who always critiqued and poked and prodded at each sermon I delivered and every action I performed on the altar. I pray that they will forgive me for the times when I fought some of them, insisting in my foolishness that I was right and they were wrong. I was young and acted like a youngster. But in all of it, I learned so much from them and pray that just as they did in the past, they will see how critical their advice is to me now.

> **When I was a child, I talked like a child, I thought like a child, I reasoned like a child. When I became a man, I put the ways of childhood behind me. 1 Corinthians 13:11 (NIV)**

As a priest, it cannot be my portion that I will be one of those who will make God's portion a desolate wilderness. And so as the Akan proverb says, *"Nea ɔreyi kwan nnim sɛ n'akyi akyea"* (The one creating the path doesn't know that the path he has cut is crooked). In essence it is the one who walks behind the one making the path, who can tell that the path is crooked. Those who have stood behind and ensured that my way is not crooked include Kofi Boateng, who took me to the Full Gospel Business Men's Fellowship International and introduced me to the idea of corporate people taking God seriously. Kofi continues to encourage me to embrace both worlds without fear or favor.

> **Many pastors have destroyed my vineyard, they have trodden my portion under foot, they have made my pleasant portion a desolate wilderness. Jeremiah 12:10 (KJV)**

I'm grateful to Margaret-Reid Bartels, who always told me that I should take great pride in my calling and pursue it against all odds and against all opposition. And the late Justice VCRAC Crabbe, who vouched for me as a referee when I applied to seminary and gave me numerous books, which have been a rich source of information for my sermons and other writings I work on.

There were a set of people who were always very frank and brutally honest with me like my brother Kwafo Ofori-Boateng, my friends Serwah Asafo Adjaye, Kwame Graham, Gordon Quartey, and Reverend Kweku Winful. And of course my coach and counselor, Sika Twum. I pray that they will continue to keep me grounded.

I cannot exclude my seminary classmates, now priests, like Reverend Dr. Lawrence Laryea, Reverend Marian Addo and Reverend Captain Emmanuel Darko, who always teased me because I was the only seminarian who was adamant that I would never become a priest!! I know now that all that laughing and teasing was just to encourage me to step into my life's purpose.

Then there are the seasoned priests like Reverend Franklin Idan, Reverend Ekow Acquah, Reverend Father Daniel Tettedji, Dean Addo, Canon Torgbor, Dean Sackey, His Grace the Most Reverend Dr. Justice Ofei Akrofi, the Right Reverend Dr. Daniel Sylvanus Mensah Torto, and of course Canon Samuel Lanquaye Lamptey who held my hand and guided me into priesthood by praying with me, discussing Scripture with me and giving me insight into the life, joys and challenges of priesthood.

Aunty Ruby Ankrah - my Godmother, Kwame Acquah, Uncle Fiifi and Aunty Philipa Dadzie, the Fynns, Aunty Regina Morrison, Aunty Aggie Agyepong (Aggie Kusi!), Aunty Abigail Amoah, and Aunty Joyce Boateng are just a few of the people who have known me since before I was eight and have taken great delight and pride in my priesthood journey. They have been an incredible source of encouragement.

I owe a big debt of gratitude to my St. Anthony family. The congregation made up of people who tolerated, forgave and corrected all my 'new preacher gaffes.' I can never show enough gratitude for the way they stood behind me and encouraged me down this path. I pray, that even though they are not my regular congregation now, they will not leave me. As fallible as I am, now is the time I need them and all my congregations to pray for me the most.

> **So guard your hearts. Be true shepherds over all the flock and feed them well. Remember, it was the Holy Spirit who appointed you to guard and oversee the churches that belong to Jesus, the Anointed One, which he purchased and established by his own blood. Acts 20:28 (TPT)**

Finally, to my mother! My mother is the one person to whom I have the most difficulty saying thank you, because I am afraid that my words cannot sufficiently express the depth of my gratitude to her. I made many mistakes with her, the greatest of them probably being that I did not trust her enough to tell her all the things I was struggling with. But despite my mistrust, her love for me never wavered. Today, she is my biggest fan and critic, I am both humbled and honored that she is my mother. My constant prayer is that God will grant her strength to see me grow in my priesthood, and that who I have become and will be, will always bring her honor and joy.

> **Strength and honor are her clothing; and she shall rejoice in time to come. Proverbs 31:25 (KJV)**

BROKEN FOR USE

Ordination for me has by no means been a destination. It has marked the beginning of a lifelong journey, and the beginning of a story in which everyone mentioned in this book has had a part to play. One person I have not mentioned is a South African friend I made while I was at Bulk. He found the concept of my going into the priesthood very fascinating but explained to me that he was not really into the whole 'God thing.' It reminded me of my chats with Ambily.

I decided to pray about it and every once in a while I would send him a short prayer or a bible passage with an explanation of the scripture on WhatsApp. Initially, I was very uncomfortable sending him these messages because I myself don't like to be bombarded with religious messages.

One day he called and said, "I like these messages, I hope you're sending them to everyone you know. I think more people should read them." In typical me style I ignored what again turned out to be God speaking. But I conceded a little and started sending them to my brother and a few close friends. I would send these messages typically by 6:00 a.m. at the very latest.

One day, I overslept and decided to skip the message. To my amazement, several people called and asked why they hadn't received it. It turned out some of my friends had been sending them to their friends and it had become their ritual to read my messages every morning. That day, another friend, Zubida, called and scolded me about how I needed to recognize that people really depended on receiving these messages.

But she went a step further and said, "And it needs to be more professionally done. It needs to be a blog!" It wasn't really a suggestion. It was more of an instruction. And to put her money where her mouth was, she suggested a few names for the name of my blog. I chose "Broken for Use."

That night she sent me the fully paid for domain name, brokenforuse.com.

If the kickoff for Jesus ministry was His mother instructing Him to turn water into wine, then the kickoff to my ministry was Zubida buying me that Broken for Use url. And I am forever grateful to her.

It made me see that as a priest I have an opportunity to make a meaningful difference in people's lives far beyond my duties in church. After a year, Zubida pulled up the statistics on the blog and showed me that it is being read in over a hundred and twenty countries. Today I get messages from people all over the world telling me how much the messages benefit them.

I have found that the novelty of a young woman being an Anglican priest has afforded me the opportunity to speak on several youth and women's platform. I have been able to use my story to encourage hundreds of young people. To make them see they can be anything they want to be, as long as they set their minds to it and put their trust in God.

I live for those seminars, because I see first-hand the eyes of young people, especially young women, light up when they realize that there is so much hope for them. They see that I am just an ordinary girl like them and have struggled with the same things they struggle with and yet God has found a way to use me. This is the reason I believe Jesus held up His hands to show the disciples after He resurrected. To show them that despite the damage to His hands and His side, He was still standing. He was still strong. And without that damage, without that crucifixion, He could not have resurrected and fulfilled His purpose - the salvation of the world.

> **When the disciples were together, with the doors locked for fear of the Jewish leaders, Jesus came and stood among them and said, "Peace be with you!" After he said this, he showed them his hands and side. The disciples were overjoyed when they saw the Lord. Again Jesus said, "Peace be with you! As the Father has sent me, I am sending you." John 20:19-21 (NIV)**

I believe that just like Jesus, we can each resurrect from our struggle. We can resurrect from rape, from addiction, from divorce and from whatever else has plagued us. And when through Christ we have overcome our difficulties, He sends us out to show our scars to others, to let them know that there is life after the scars. And that life is good.

My life now is a far cry from the misery of my secondary school and university days. As a worker priest, I shuttle constantly between engineering work, priestly work, and family life. And what I have discovered is that they are actually one and the same thing. All work is from God and must be done for Him. So whether its sick visitations, swimming with my daughter, or debating with other engineers about what design we should use, I consult God and I feel His presence.

As a priest, my day typically begins at 4:00 a.m. when I pray, and write my daily Broken for Use blog. If I am scheduled for morning Mass, then it means I need to be at the Cathedral by 5:30 a.m. to celebrate the Mass. I love those early morning drives to church. Just like in my secondary school days, that is still when I have some of my heartiest chats with God. And that's when I make deals with Him. Immediately after the one-hour morning Mass, I rush to GIS to catch my daughter and pray for her before she starts school. From then on I switch into engineering mode, unless I have sick visitations or counselling sessions with someone. I have several young people especially women that I counsel and they are the reason this book has become necessary. To serve as an instrument to help the many more whom I may not be able to reach personally.

When I first embarked on this priesthood journey, I was warned severally by non-orthodox Christians that the Anglican Church would limit me. But they could not have been more wrong. The Anglican Church has afforded me a huge platform. Supported by the Church, my foundation, Aequitas – A Fairer World, has allowed me to work with underprivileged youth to help balance some of the imbalances in our society, especially around youth health and youth education. We have clothed hundreds of destitute children all over the country and recently began a campaign to raise funds for childhood cancer which in Ghana is not covered by health insurance.

When I look at how God is using me now, it makes me sorry that I wasted so many years fretting over being divorced. I praise God that unlike me, the Anglican Church, looked upon me not as a divorcee who needed to be condemned but as a child of God, who, like all children of God, has sinned and fallen short of the glory of God. Divorce damaged me, but I want to assure you that, whatever has damaged you, has already done its worst. Christ overcame death in order that all of us can overcome. There is life after damage. And that life is not a life of misery and condemnation. That life is a life of thriving and joy and purpose.

Through our brokenness, we become useful vessels.

I love being an Anglican priest. God was right. Priesthood is my calling. Every day I wake up, I thank Him for not giving up on me. Right now, I have no idea what lies ahead of me but, I'm excited about whatever it is and my constant prayer is found in this hymn by Isaac Williams:

BE THOU my Guardian and my Guide,
And hear me when I call;
Let not my slippery footsteps slide,
And hold me lest I fall.

The world, the flesh and Satan dwell
Around the path I tread,
O save me from the snares of hell,
Thou Quickener of the dead.

And if I tempted am to sin,
And outward things are strong,
Do Thou, O Lord, keep watch within
And save my soul from wrong.

Still let me ever watch and pray,
And feel that I am frail;
That if the Tempter cross my way,
Yet he may not prevail.